10 STEPS TO BECOME A SUCCESSFUL STUDENT ENTREPRENEUR

why the world's most successful entrepreneurs started in school and why you can too

RICHARD ANNAN

10 STEPS TO BECOME A

SUCCESSFUL STUDENT ENTREPRENEUR

WHY THE WORLD GREATEST ENTREPRENEURS STARTED IN SCHOOL AND HOW YOU CAN TOO

RICHARD ANNAN

TABLE OF CONTENT

STEPS	DETAILS	PAGE
STEP 1	**BECOME A STUDENT ENTREPRENEUR:** All you need to know about entrepreneurship before you start	5
STEP 2	**IDENTIFY BUSINESS OPPORTUNITIES** 100 business opportunities for young entrepreneurs	26
STEP 3	**VALIDATE YOUR BUSINESS IDEAS** Ensure your business idea will sell before you start	40
STEP 4	**DEVELOP CORE SKILLS** Develop skills that will make you succeed	48
STEP 5	**CREATE PARTNERSHIP** Connect with the right people for business success	58
STEP 6	**START SMALL - BEAT THE INEXPERIENCE BARRIER** Overcome the Student Entrepreneur Greatest Challenge	68
STEP 7	**MAKE THE SALE** Learn strategies to sell and market your products	81
STEP 8	**RAISE CAPITAL** Mobilize Resource to Start and Grow your Business	94
STEP 9	**PREPARE A BUSINESS PLAN** Develop a success blueprint to help you grow your business	106
STEP 10	**REGISTER YOUR BUNINESS** Complete all Legal Requirement for Your New Business	128
FINAL WORD	**LET ACHIEVE TOGETHER**	136

MORE RESOURCE AT RICHARDANNAN.COM

As a young entrepreneur, you have made the right decision by reading the '10 Steps to Become a Successful Student Entrepreneur'. This book contains resource that will guide every student or young entrepreneur to succeed as an entrepreneur.

The author, Richard Annan started as a student entrepreneur and has acquired more than twenty years' experience as an author, speaker, entrepreneur and banking executive, working with businesses and providing business advisory services on Banking, Finance, Technology and Digital Marketing.

If you require more guidance, mentorship, support and advise on your success journey as a young entrepreneur, visit richardannan.com and sign up for Richard's Free Webinars for Personal and Business Growth.

Richard Annan
Speaker I Author I Entrepreneur I Business Executive

STEP 1

BECOME A STUDENT ENTREPREURS:

ALL YOU NEED TO KNOW ABOUT ENTREPRENEURSHIP BEFORE YOU START YOUR BUSINESS

The world is made up of two people; Business owners and employees. When you are a business owner, you take a lot of risk. When you are an employee, you take less risk. Wealth and financial rewards are distributed based on which of these two divisions you belong to. Figure 1:1 show the two division of the world.

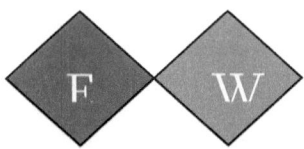

FIGURE 1.1: WEALTH DISTRIBUTION QUADRANT

Those at the left side of the quadrant (The E Quadrant) are business owners. The world knows them as entrepreneurs. The Entrepreneurs Quadrant is made up of people who starts and own their own businesses and corporations.

The right side of the quadrant (The W Quadrant) is made up of workers or employees of businesses and corporations (Figure 1.2) that work for Entrepreneurs.

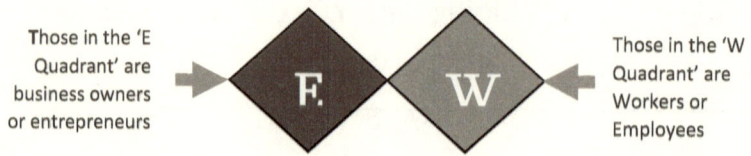

FIGURE 1.2: THE LEFT AND RIGHT SIDE OF THE WEALTH DISTRIBUTION QUADRANT

This division is responsible for allocating resource and wealth for people in the world.

This concept of classification was popularized by Karl Marx who saw the world as a constant struggle between the property-owning class (upper class or bourgeoisie) and the working class (proletariat). According to Karl Marx, the world is divided into two class or people. Those who own the means of production and those who do not own any means of production. In other words, you are either in the class of entrepreneurs or you are not.

This book is about those in the' E Quadrant' or those who want to be in the 'E Quadrant' of the Wealth Distribution Quadrant. It's about how people can embrace entrepreneurship and create wealth at the most vital time in history when more wealth is being created than any other time in the history of mankind.

THE 'E QUADRANT' IS THE WEALTH ORIGINATION QUADRANT

Entrepreneurs are wealth originators. They originate wealth from ideas that otherwise may have no value at all. The world's most valuable product (the iPhone) did not even exist some 20 years ago. It is the product of an idea originated and carefully launched only in 2007 by an entrepreneur who set his mind on changing the world.

Those in the 'E Quadrant' are wealth originators

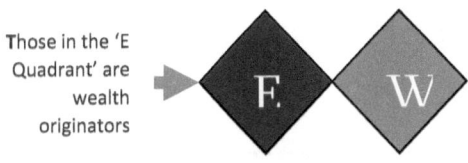

FIGURE 1.3: THE LEFT AND RIGHT SIDE OF THE WEALTH DISTRIBUTION

Every successful entrepreneur is also a successful dreamer. You must clearly develop and know where you want to go before you set off. The extent to which you believe in your idea or dream will determine the level of commitment or sacrifice you are willing to make to make that idea becomes a reality.

The commitment or sacrifice an entrepreneur makes in order to actualize his ideas is called Equity. The world defines equity as a business owner's stake or contribution to the business. This sacrifice is in the form of time, money, lands and other resources or factors of production which the entrepreneur brings together in order to implement his ideas. Without these sacrifices no business will exist and no wealth will be created.

When an entrepreneur is successful, he is able to transform his idea into quantifiable products or service which returns him profit. He creates wealth which becomes his reward for starting his business.

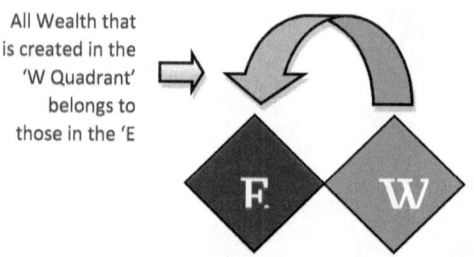

All Wealth that is created in the 'W Quadrant' belongs to those in the 'E

FIGURE 1.4: WEALTH BELONGS TO THOSE IN THE 'E QUADRANT'

THE 'W QUADRANT' IS THE LABOUR QUADRANT

While the 'E Quadrant' is the wealth origination quadrant, the 'W Quadrant' is best described as the labour quadrant. The 'W Quadrant' is where work is actually done to generate wealth or profit.

All resource that an entrepreneur puts together must be put to use by labor or employees who are in the 'W Quadrant'. Every wealth that is generated in the 'W Quadrant' however belongs to those in the 'E Quadrant' (Figure 1.4).

When a shop makes profits, these profits belong to the owners of the shop not the employees. The Entrepreneur at all-time lays claim to whatever wealth the employee creates because he is responsible for originating the Wealth Distribution Quadrant which is generating the wealth or profit. He is the originator of the idea which has resulted in the wealth being created.

IF BEING AN ENTREPRENEUR IS SO REWARDING WHY ARENT ALL OF US ENTREPRENEURS?

Becoming an entrepreneur doesn't come at a cheap price, which explains why most of us are not entrepreneurs anyway. First, entrepreneurs take a great risk bringing together the various factors of production in order to start their business. They may ran at a loss and lose their investment if their startup fail. The sacrifice

they make may include denying themselves so much pleasure at the start of their business in order to push every little resource they have into their business. Even

so, statistics indicates 25% of all startups fail in their first year. Entrepreneurs must therefore be able to embrace and manage risk in order to succeed. Employees however take less risk and will not suffer any such losses. They take less risk and so it is much easier for most of us to go by that route.

Because becoming an employee comes with less risk, society takes the safety-first approach by preparing us to be employees instead preparing us to be entrepreneurs. As a child my parent always encouraged me to get good grades at school so I can find a good job once I graduate from the University.

Again, the university trains you to study and then look for a blue color job once you graduate. Our society is been set up to encourage you to learn so you can work for someone later, and not to start a business for yourself. Most university programs won't encourage you to start your own business and mentor you to succeed. Instead, most of our university/college students require taking an internship as requirement for the course of study. The whole educational system is just one big program that is designed to prepare us to work for someone else instead of preparing us to work for ourselves.

WHAT IS STUDENT ENTREPRENEURSHIP?

Student entrepreneurship refers to the practice of students starting and managing their own businesses while still pursuing their education. It involves identifying opportunities, developing innovative ideas, and creating sustainable ventures with the goal of achieving financial independence and making a positive impact. Student entrepreneurship encompasses a wide range of activities, from launching tech startups and e-commerce ventures to providing freelance services and running small-scale businesses on campus.

What distinguishes student entrepreneurship from traditional forms of entrepreneurship is the fact that it typically occurs within the context of higher education. Students who engage in entrepreneurship often juggle their academic coursework with the demands of running a business, requiring them to balance their time and priorities effectively.

Student entrepreneurs may leverage their university resources, such as mentorship programs, business incubators, and networking events, to support their entrepreneurial endeavors. They also have the opportunity to apply the knowledge and skills gained in the classroom to real-world challenges, fostering experiential learning and personal growth.

In recent years, there has been a noticeable surge in the number of students venturing into entrepreneurship while still pursuing their education. This trend reflects a significant shift in the traditional perception of career paths and underscores the growing recognition of the value of entrepreneurial endeavors among the youth. Student entrepreneurship is not merely about starting a business; it represents a mindset characterized by innovation, resilience, and a thirst for learning.

The rise of student entrepreneurship can be attributed to several factors. Firstly, the accessibility of resources and information in today's digital age has lowered the barriers to entry for aspiring entrepreneurs. With the proliferation of online learning platforms, incubators, and networking opportunities, students now have unprecedented access to knowledge and support systems conducive to entrepreneurship.

Moreover, the changing landscape of the job market has prompted many students to seek alternative paths to secure their future. The allure of autonomy, flexibility, and the potential for significant financial rewards has drawn an increasing number of students towards entrepreneurship as a viable career option.

HOW SUCCESSFUL ARE STUDENTS ENTREPRENEURS?

++Microsoft, Facebook, FedEx, Dell, Apple, Yahoo are some of the most successful businesses in the world today, and all these businesses were started by student entrepreneurs while still in school or after school. In fact, some of the most successful entrepreneurs either started in school or prepared themselves actively whiles in school. The list of successful students' entrepreneurs also runs parallel to the list of the worlds richest. We discuss a few of the most successful entrepreneurs who started their business whiles in school.

BILL GATES AND MICROSOFT: Bill Gates is the richest man in the world, with a net worth of about $125.5 billion as at March 2024. Whiles still a student at Harvard, Bill Gates teamed up with his friend Paul Allen to start a business with an idea of creating computer processors and interfaces that continues to have wide application in computing today. Bill Gates will soon leave Harvard to start his company Microsoft, which will dominate the computing business for several decades. His computing business has expanded into video games, mobile phones, and hardware and search engine optimization.

MUBARAK MAYIKA AND ZAGRACE: Mayika is the most promising student entrepreneur in tech from Kenya. Mubarak Mayika founded a web hosting company called Hypercentury Technologies when he was only 16 years old. After operating the company for two years, Mayika sold the company to Wamp Telecom for an undisclosed amount. He then started a new venture called Zagrace after successfully raising venture funding from local investors. Zagrace is cloud based enterprise software that helps companies manage their inventory, payroll, marketing and other aspect of their operations.

MARK ZUCKERBERG AND FACEBOOK: Whiles in school Mark Zuckerberg started coding what will become known as Facebook today. His incredible rise to riches and his youthfulness makes him one of the most inspirational student entrepreneurs alive today. Zuckerberg launched Facebook in his Harvard dormitory room in February 4, 2004, which is a now a listed company on the New York Stock Exchange with over $134 billion in annual revenue and assets in excess of $800 billion as at March 2024.

MABEL SUGLO AND ECO SHOES: While studying at the School of Allies Health Sciences at the University of Development Studies in Ghana, Mabel Suglo co-founded Eco Shoes Social Enterprise that manufacturer shoes and sandals and offers skilled training and job opportunities to disabled and other youth in Ghana. She partnered Jachai School in the Ashanti region of Ghana to train more than 500 disabled on how to produce shoes using local waste materials such as car tyres. Mabel's has been hugely successful, and she has been recognized by media houses such as BBC, Rising Africa, and Leaders-Afrique.

FRAZER DOHERTY AND SUPERJAM: While schooling, Frazer Doherty started making jams at the age of 14 years using his grandmother's recipe. From a humble beginning at a Scottish village, Doherty grew his business from his mother's kitchen to major shelves of retailers all over the world. His business SuperJam grew into global brands by the time he was 16. SuperJam now supplies over 2000 supermarkets across the world including Tesco, WalMart, Waitrose, Morrison, Sainsbury and Asda. He was awarded the 2007 Global Student Entrepreneur Award and Outstanding Young person of the World Award in addition to several other awards. SuperJam is exhibited at the National Museum of Scotland as an 'Iconic Scottish Brand'.

FREDERIK W. SMITH AND FEDEX: while studying at Yale University, Frederick W. Smith wrote a research paper on how courier and delivery Service Company can be successful in the information age. Smith will later apply his research findings to a real-world company he bought in 1970, transforming the aviation repair company he acquired into a worldwide courier and delivery service company. FedEx is now $90.2 billion annual revenue business with a total asset in excess of $87 billion as at December 2023.

RAINDOLF OWUSU AND OASIS WEBSOFT: At 21 years, a student of Methodist University College in Ghana founded Oasis Websoft, a fledgling web and applications development company. Oasis Websoft successfully launched its own web browser in addition to running an online school teaching Website Development. Raindolf Owusu was honored as a 2015 Washington Mandela Fellow by President Barack Obama. He was also honored as a Guido Sohne Fellow by the Free and Open Source Foundation for Africa (FOSSFA) in Abuja, Nigeria.

MICHAEL DELL AND DELL INC.: While a pre-med student at University of Texas, Dell started a small computer repair and upgrade business in his dormitory selling IBM computers. He later dropped out of school to focus fully on his fledgling business after receiving $1,000.00 loan from his family for expansion. Dell expanded into a multinational corporation employing more than 100,000 staff worldwide. The company is now a $91.1 billion revenue per year business (as at December 2023) providing a broad range of technology solutions for consumer, education, healthcare, enterprise and government sectors.

STEVE JOBS AND APPLE: In 1971, Steve Wozniak who enrolled at the University of California teamed up with his friend Steve Jobs to build 'blue boxes' that enabled people to make long distance calls. Their project will eventually transform into the world most valuable brand. Apple is today the world largest technology company by asset, and the world 2nd largest company by revenue and in addition to being the world largest publicly traded company in the world in 2014, it also became the first company to be valued at over $700 billion.

SEAN BELNICK AND BIZCHAIR.COM: While walking around his father's furniture shop, Belnick made one important observation. Potential clients will call his dad shop, ask about his product and come to his shop to have a look at these products. Why not save these clients the long trip to the stores. Sean Belnick started bizchair.com as an online furniture shop. Belnick launched this company with just $500.00 from his bedroom at the age of 16 with the help of his father who will help him with the administration of the website once he closes from school. By the time he turned 20 years, bizchair.com was worth $24 million with clients including Microsoft, Google and the Pentagon.

CAMERON JOHNSON AND CERTIFICATESWAP.COM: As early as 9years, Cameron Johnson started his first business selling gift cards and invitation cards to his friends. Johnson will later start another business selling baby dolls on ebay. He made his first $50,000.00 which he invested in another business, surfingprize.com by the time he was 13 years old. He hired coders and programmers to work on surfingprize.com, an online ad company that scrolls advertisement at the top of your browser whenever you are online. His company was worth $1 million with annual revenue of $3.6 million by the time he turned 19 years. After High School, Cameron Johnson enrolled at Virginia Polytechnic Institute. Johnson again started certificateswap.com which he will sell in 2004 for an undisclosed amount.

JAMES MURRAY WELLS AND GLASSES DIRECT: Whiles studying English at the University of West London, Wells visited an optician who recommended he buy a pair of new glasses. After a brief shop around and realizing the glasses were so expensive, he contacted a manufacturer and discovered a pair glasses selling for £150.00 only cost £7.00 to make. James Murray wells then launched his own online business selling glasses using what remained of his student's loan as startup capital. In only his first year, Glasses Direct raked in $1 million selling 22,000 pair of spectacles. By 2009, Glasses Direct was selling a pair of glasses every 3 minutes and had more than 70 employees. The business was sold in 2014 with annual revenue of $34 million.

JERRY YANG, DAVID FILO AND YAHOO: As graduate students in 1994 at Stanford University, Jerry Yang and David Filo created a website that consisted of directory and index of other websites to aid them surf the worldwide web more easily. As the site became more popular, they renamed it to Yahoo! Inc. Yahoo has become one of the most popular websites in the world. It is ranked as the most read news and media website with over 7 billion readers per month in addition to being the fourth most visited website globally. Yahoo is also listed on the New York Stock Exchange with $4.61 billion annual revenue and total asset of $61.9 billion in 2014.

ANDREW FASHION AND MYSPACESUPPORT.COM: Not all successful student entrepreneur stories have a happy ending. Some successful students' entrepreneurs end up preempting their own failure. Such is the case of Andrew Fashion who made $2 million dollars by the time he was 21 years and blew it all before he turned 22 years. In his 6th grade, Andrew figured a way to transform their pencils into miniature rocket launchers which he sold to other students in school. He started a business called Flaming Gold and operated it at the school till the school banned his pencils. Andrew then started myspacesupport.com in 2005, which was earning him more than $100,000.00 every month in advertising revenue. But after a few years of living a high life, Andrew blew all his earnings on gambling and women whiles the revenue from his business also dried up, causing him to fall from being a millionaire to being in debt. Andrew is working hard to promote another business he started called BeModel.com. He is also authoring his biography, which wills details his rise and fall which he has titled 'Young and Stupid'.

DO ALL STUDENTS STARTUP SUCCEED? OF COURSE NOT!

Of course, not all student startups succeed and not all non-student startups succeed too. In fact, anyone who wants to become an entrepreneur must have a knack for failure. Failure or setbacks are a constant part of being an entrepreneur, and comes readily with the terrain.

Every successful entrepreneur has had an experience of having to overcoming tremendous setbacks and failure along the way; Potential customers will say no. Reliable partners will give up on you. Sales will not come as expected. Conflicts and power struggles will arise where you least expect. The economy will grow from bad to worse to downright hostile and sales will plummet. Your bank will refuse your credit request and you will end up losing out on your most anticipated contract. This is the risk you take once you become an entrepreneur, so you must learn to accept 'no!' with grace numerous times and still have the courage to work on till the 'yes' that will be your breakthrough arrives. If you give up after any rejection, setback or no, you forfeit your right to success. Your ability to face and overcome setbacks will determine whether you succeed or not.

REASONS FOR STARTUP FAILURES

About 25% of all startups fail within one year of operation. 50% of all startup fold up by their 4th year of operation. Reasons for such failures are near and wide, the major one being attributed largely to incompetence.

THE TEAM DOESN'T HAVE THE REQUIRED SKILLS: 46% of all startup failures can be attributed to incompetence, which is to say the team does not have what it takes to succeed in their chosen business. One of the most profound challenges faced by startups is how to get their team right. Top level financiers and venture funds always want to be certain those behind a company are capable of delivering results. A good entrepreneur will look for partners that complement his weakness and add value to the company as a whole.

PRODUCT DOESN'T SERVE ANY DEFINED MARKET: Business is subject to the classic economic law of demand and supply. There must be a clear demand for your product or service for your startup to survive. Without a clearly defined market need from your product or supply, your startup has no chance of survival. Most business has folded up simply due to the non-existence of demand for their product. An idea may look good, a product may be nice, but that doesn't guarantee the market will accept it. Merely identifying a product you can produce or a service you can offer is not a guarantee for jackpot. Most importantly you must have an in-depth understanding of your market even where there is an obvious demand for your product. Who are you competitors and why do clients' patronize the product/service. If you don't understand where you are going, you will probably end up somewhere else.

POOR CASHFLOW MANAGEMENT: Many a student entrepreneur aiming to climb the success ladder, there is one rule you should never forget. Cash is king! Without it, your new startup will grind to a sudden halt. This is the reality of most startup that fails when their startup cash dries up. As a student entrepreneur you must quickly abreast yourself with the importance of maintaining constant liquidity in your new business.

Businesses that fail in this manner are not necessarily insolvent. They miscalculate and invest their cash in areas that are less pressing such as renting a bigger office when you could do with a smaller office, employing staff you do not need, stocking up raw materials you may not necessarily need now, paying upfront for everything when you could negotiate for a discount or get suppliers credit. You must know that once you ran out of cash, the very survival of your company will be threatened.

POOR CUSTOMER MANAGEMENT: A happy customer makes a successful company. Your customer's subjective valuation of your business will determine whether your business will survive or fail. Forget about how nice or useful your product is or how well you believe it will meet their needs. Your clients are the only one that determines the extent to which your products satisfy their needs. Once they think you are not meeting their need, your business will be fighting for survival. I have had several experiences where entrepreneurs have taken their client's for granted and have paid a dear price for it. One such company (ABZ Company) was a contractor for a major state institution. On one instance it supplied substandard goods to the state institution which refused to take delivery of the goods due to the fact that it doesn't meet their standard and further cancelled future contracts to his ABZ Company. The state institution was the major client for ABZ Company and cancelling futures business affected cashflow and caused ABZ to default on loans it has taken from its bankers. The company finally went insolvent in 2013. Your customer's valuation of your products/services is the intangible asset that keeps your business afloat. Poor customer management causes many businesses to fail.

BECOMING AN ENTREPRENEUR TO BECOME RICH: This is an important benefit for entrepreneurs but let it stay as a benefit. Don't let becoming rich be the main reason you are in business. Many businesses have failed simply because monetary gains are the driving focus of their business. Such misplaced focus will affect every aspect of your business including how you treat your clients, how you price your products/service and the value you deliver to your clients.

HOW DO YOU BENFIT FROM BECOMING A STUDENTS ENTREPRENEUR

While becoming a student entrepreneur doesn't come on a silver platter, entrepreneurship offers several benefits that make the calling worthwhile.

YOU DO WHAT YOU LOVE: As a KNUST student in 2006, I founded the Business Development Foundation to encourage other students to become entrepreneurs. It was a passion I have had all my life. Organising entrepreneurship seminars also meant I got to meet a lot of prominent people which I enjoyed the most. I was making positive impact in the life of people all around me and I loved it. As a student entrepreneur, you get to choose what kind of business you want to do which is never the case when you work for someone else. Doing work that makes you happy is one of the greatest gifts you can ever receive from becoming an entrepreneur.

FLEXIBILITY: Entrepreneurs create their own business which means they get to organize their time and work schedule as they like it. Having your own business means you can choose to work from 1am to 5pm instead working to a strict timeline when you are working at someone else's company.

GAIN VALUABLE EXPERIENCE: As a young entrepreneur, you get to learn how you can manage and grow your own business, gaining indispensable knowledge and experience throughout the whole process.

GARNER SUPPORTS AND MOBILISE STARTUP FUNDS: As a student, you are more likely to gain the support and help of your parents, guardians and family when running your own business. Many student entrepreneurs start their business with the help of relatives and friends who are willing to invest in their business. Others start by setting up their first office in their parents' house or garages which save them from incurring rents and other fixed cost at the start of their business. When you are a student, parent and other relative feels they have an obligation to cater for your need which means you are in a much better position to garner their support and mobilise resources to start your business. One great challenge I faced organising my first seminar was raising enough capital to pay for the speaker's fee. After speaking unsuccessfully to two finance houses, I finally spoke to my dad who gracefully borrowed GHS1,000.00 from Tech Credit Union in Kumasi for me to pay the invited speakers 2006. When I spoke to him about my business and how I invested every money I had into the business, he was very willing to help. Once you graduate from school, parent and other relatives may not feel the same sense of obligation to help you in your business as they may do when you are still in school, which is the more reason why you should start your business now.

WIDENED JOB OPPORTUNITIES: One important benefit you derive from becoming a student entrepreneur is the option it presents you after leaving school. You now have two choices; either to continue your business or look for another job whiles your employees manages your business for you. Students who do not start their business have no other choice than to go on the odious road of looking for employment which can be quite frustrating especially where they do not have any relevant work experience.

DIVERSIFY YOUR INCOME: Every student eagerly awaits that day when he/she finally graduates and start earning some income. But wouldn't it be awesome living that life now? While other students may rely on student's loans to fund their education, you could begin earning income from starting a small business which could also save you from graduating college with debts.

FINANCIAL FREEDOM: Many students entrepreneurs who continue to operate their business after school will simply learn the fact that entrepreneurship is the certain path to financial freedom. While not every entrepreneur will succeed, it still stands as the most definite sure way to generate adequate income if you want to achieve your financial freedom.

FOUR QUESTIONS TO ASK BEFORE STARTING YOUR BUSINESS

WHO ARE MY CLIENTS/WHAT ARE THEIR NEEDS? Your business will exist to serve customers and will cease to exist if there are not enough customers who want your product. In your mind you may see a clear need for your product and a very good reason why you will use such a product. But can you identify target market with enough demand to be able to operate a profitable business serving their needs? If you can't identify a specific market that will use your business or service it will be best to move to a different idea with a proven market.

What problems will you be solving for your clients and will your clients be willing to pay for your services? It is important your idea can generate enough sales to enable you operate a successful business.

WHAT IS THE COST IN ENTERING INTO SUCH A BUSINESS: Many world class businesses were started with little capital. Some started in school dormitories and garages while others with no permanent office at all. Nonetheless, it is important you know exactly what will be required if you want to enter into your chosen business. Will you need any special equipment, software or employee to start? What are the costs of raw material and do you have to incur storage cost? This information will make you take informed decisions on your startup and avoid folding up for lack of funds.

DO YOU HAVE A PASSION FOR IT? Successful entrepreneurs are passionate about their business. They set up their business around what they love to do and are motivated to work even when they don't receive the reward they expect. If you have to start a business, you should ensure you have passion for whatever business you want to do. A passionate sales person will continue knocking on doors even when customers say no. A passionate artist will practice and practice till his skills are incomparable. A passionate fashion designer can work for 18 hours and still want to work more hours for the love of his/her business. Passions is a common denominator of all successful entrepreneurs, and is the driving force that pushes them to succeed.

WILL YOUR BUSINESS BE LEGAL: If you are thinking of operating a drinking spot, you should be mindful the law doesn't allow anyone below the age of 18 years to drink not alone operate a drinking spot. Some businesses will require obtaining special license or even professional certification and can put you at the wrong side of the law if you start operating such businesses without obtaining the required licenses. If you have any doubt about the businesses you want to start, you should speak to a legal advisor if you have access to such services. You can also discuss with a senior person in the same line of business or do research further about it on the internet.

STEP 2

IDENTIFY BUSINESS OPPORTUNITIES

100 BUSINESS OPPORTUNITIES FOR YOUNG ENTREPRENEURS

The ability to identify and seize business opportunities stands as a cornerstone of success in the world of entrepreneurship. Identifying the right business opportunities lets you know which business to starts, which sector to targets, who to target for sales, and when to even start the business.

I will briefly explain the meaning of Business Opportunity and elaborate on how young entrepreneurs can identify business opportunities. In the final section of this chapter, I will list 100 business opportunities that young entrepreneurs can adopt to start their business.

Business opportunities refer to favorable situations that present potential for growth, profitability, and competitive advantage in the marketplace. These opportunities can arise from various sources, including technological advancements, market needs, lifestyle changes, or global economic shifts. Understanding what constitutes a business opportunity, why it's crucial to recognize them, and how to identify potential goldmines are vital steps on the path to entrepreneurial achievement.

THE SIGNIFICANCE OF IDENTIFYING BUSINESS OPPORTUNITIES

The importance of identifying business opportunities cannot be overstated. It is the cornerstone of entrepreneurship and innovation, leading to the creation of value, employment, and societal progress. Recognizing and seizing these opportunities allow businesses to gain a competitive edge, expand into new markets, and achieve sustainable growth. Moreover, in an era characterized by rapid change, the ability to adapt and capitalize on emerging trends is critical for long-term success. To elaborate further, let focus on two of the most successful student entrepreneurs of our lifetime.

GATES AND THE COMPUTER REVOLUTION

Bill Gates, co-founder of Microsoft who started as a student entrepreneur, exemplifies how identifying and seizing a business opportunity at the right time can lead to unparalleled success. In the mid-1970s, Gates recognized the potential of personal computing, a nascent industry at the time. He foresaw that computers would become an indispensable part of every home and office, transforming the way people work, communicate, and entertain themselves.

The opportunity materialized when IBM, seeking an operating system for its first personal computer, approached Microsoft. Gates secured a deal to provide the operating system, MS-DOS, despite Microsoft not owning one at the time. This move not only solved IBM's immediate need but also positioned Microsoft at the forefront of the software industry. Gates' ability to identify the potential of personal computing and act decisively paved the way for Microsoft's dominance in the software market.

MARK ZUCKERBERG AND THE RISE OF SOCIAL NETWORKING

Similarly, Mark Zuckerberg is another student entrepreneur whose ability to identify business opportunities lead to phenomenal success. Mark Zuckerberg's creation of Facebook stemmed from recognizing the opportunity to enhance connectivity and social interaction among college students. Initially launched at Harvard University, Facebook rapidly expanded to other colleges and eventually to the general public. Zuckerberg identified a universal desire for people to connect and share their lives online, a need that was unmet by existing services at the time.

Facebook's success lies in Zuckerberg's vision of a more connected world and his understanding of the social dynamics among its users. By continually evolving the platform to incorporate new features such as news feed, photo sharing, and live streaming, Facebook has maintained its relevance and dominance in the social media landscape.

HOW TO IDENTIFY BUSINESS OPPORTUNITIES

Identifying business opportunities is both an art and a science. It involves a keen observation of the market, understanding consumer behaviour, and staying abreast of technological advancements. Student entrepreneurs must master this science and art. It forms the foundation to every business idea, every personal or social enterprise. Here are key strategies to identify business opportunities:

MARKET RESEARCH: Research plays a pivotal role in understanding market dynamics, customer needs, and emerging trends, providing a solid foundation for business decisions. The story of FedEx, the global courier delivery services company, serves as a powerful example of how research can be instrumental in identifying and capitalizing on business opportunities.

The inception of FedEx can be traced back to a college research paper written by Frederick W. Smith, the company's founder, while he was a student at Yale University. In his paper, Smith outlined a business model for an overnight delivery service in a computer information age. He recognized the inefficiencies in the current delivery system, where shipments were routed through centralized hubs, causing delays. This insight was born out of thorough research and understanding of the logistics and transportation industry's challenges at the time.

After graduating, Smith took his academic insights into the real world, leading to the formation of FedEx. FedEx continued to invest heavily in market research to understand customer needs and expectations after its formation. This ongoing process helped FedEx to tailor its services to meet the evolving demands of businesses worldwide, such as the introduction of tracking technology and guaranteed next-day delivery in specific time slots. Student entrepreneurs must learn to adopt research as a tool for identifying businesses opportunities and well as understanding market dynamics.

NETWORK AND COLLABORATE: In the dynamic world of entrepreneurship, networking is not just about building relationships; it's a strategic tool for identifying and seizing business opportunities.

For student entrepreneurs, networking can be particularly impactful, offering a unique platform to connect with mentors, investors, peers, and industry professionals. These connections can lead to collaborations, insights into market needs, and even the discovery of untapped market niches.

Networking involves more than exchanging business cards or adding contacts on LinkedIn. It's about engaging in meaningful conversations, sharing ideas, and establishing relationships with individuals who can offer insights, advice, and support. For student entrepreneurs, networking can be particularly beneficial, providing access to a wealth of knowledge and experiences that can help in navigating the complexities of starting and growing a business. Sophia Alvarez, a business student passionate about sustainable fashion, connected with peers at a university entrepreneurship club meeting who shared her vision. This network of like-minded individuals became the foundation for *EcoWear*, a startup focused on creating a platform for sustainable fashion brands. Networking within the university environment allowed her to find not just co-founders but also mentors among the faculty who guided her through the initial stages of her business. For student entrepreneurs should be intentional about using networking and collaboration to identify business opportunities.

LEVERAGE TECHNOLOGY: In the digital age, technology serves as a powerful catalyst for identifying and seizing business opportunities. It has democratized access to markets, made information more accessible, and opened new avenues for innovation. Among the most agile and innovative users of technology to identify business opportunities are student entrepreneurs. These individuals have leveraged technological tools, platforms, and data analytics to pinpoint gaps in the market and launch successful ventures.

Technology enables entrepreneurs to gather and analyze vast amounts of data, monitor trends in real-time, and engage with potential customers worldwide. Social media, online marketplaces, and digital advertising platforms offer unprecedented access to market insights. Moreover, technological tools can help validate business ideas through rapid prototyping, online surveys, and A/B testing, significantly reducing the time and resources required to test market viability.

Ben Silbermann, along with a couple of friends, launched Pinterest while he was a student. Pinterest, a visual discovery engine for finding ideas like recipes, home and style inspiration, and more, started as a simple idea. The platform leveraged technology to tap into the growing desire for a more visual and curated online experience. By identifying and acting on this emerging trend, Silbermann and his team were able to grow Pinterest into one of the most popular websites in the world, with millions of users using the platform to discover and share inspiration. Young entrepreneurs should embrace technology as a means to uncover and exploit new market opportunities, thereby shaping the future of business and innovation.

CUSTOMER FEEDBACK: Listening to customer feedback is more than a practice of good customer service; it's a strategic tool for uncovering business opportunities. In the entrepreneurial journey, especially for those just starting out, understanding the customer's voice can illuminate paths not previously considered, revealing gaps in the market ripe for innovation. This approach has been successfully leveraged by student entrepreneurs across the globe, who have turned feedback into foundational elements of their startups. Here, we explore how these enterprising individuals used customer insights to drive their business ideas, with a focus on the companies they started and the strategies they employed.

One of the most compelling examples of leveraging customer feedback is Michael Dell, the founder of Dell Technologies. While a student at the University of Texas at Austin, Dell started a business upgrading computers in his dorm room. His direct engagement with customers revealed a significant opportunity: people wanted more cost-effective, customized computer solutions. By listening to this feedback, Dell was able to refine his business model, focusing on selling directly to consumers. This direct-to-consumer model not only allowed for better customization but also reduced costs, giving Dell a competitive edge. Dell Technologies grew from a dorm room startup to a global leader in the computer industry, illustrating the power of customer feedback in shaping business strategy.

The story of Michael Dell underscores the transformative potential of customer feedback in uncovering and capitalizing on business opportunities. For student entrepreneurs, actively seeking and thoughtfully responding to customer feedback can be a game-changer, turning initial concepts into viable, growth-oriented businesses. By embracing feedback as a cornerstone of the entrepreneurial process, student founders can navigate the complexities of the market with greater confidence and clarity, laying the foundation for lasting success.

FLEXIBILITY: Be willing to pivot or adapt your business model based on new findings or changes in the market environment is critical to achieving success in todays market. The ability to pivot, adapt, and evolve in response to market feedback, emerging trends, or unforeseen challenges is what often differentiates successful ventures from those that falter.

Flexibility in the context of entrepreneurship involves the willingness to change directions, refine products or services, or even overhaul business models based on new insights or market demands. For student entrepreneurs, who may have limited resources but an abundance of creativity and resilience, being flexible allows for rapid learning and adjustment in the fast-paced world of startups. This agility can open doors to niches and markets that were previously hidden or deemed unattainable.

Evan Spiegel and Bobby Murphy initially launched an app called Picaboo, which was meant to be a disappearing-image messaging service. The initial concept did not take off as expected, leading them to reassess their approach. Learning from their initial feedback, they relaunched the app as Snapchat. This pivot not only addressed the privacy concerns associated with digital photo sharing but also tapped into the younger generation's desire for spontaneous and ephemeral communication. Snapchat's flexibility in its early days was crucial to its eventual success, transforming it into a social media giant that caters to millions of users worldwide.

By staying agile, responsive, and open to change, young entrepreneurs can navigate the complexities of the market, identifying opportunities that align with their vision and capabilities for lasting impact.

100 BUSINESS OPPORTUNITIES FOR STUDENT ENTREPRENEURS

Each of 100 business opportunities presented below can be started with relatively low initial investment, making them ideal for student entrepreneurs looking to venture into the world of business. Whether through leveraging skills in technology and design, tapping into the demand for health and wellness, or exploring the potential of sustainable and green businesses, there are ample opportunities for innovative and driven students to make their mark.

CREATIVE & MEDIA

1. **Graphic Design Services:** Offer design services for businesses or individuals.
2. **Photography:** Provide photography services for events, products, or portraits.
3. **Videography Services:** Offer video production for events or promotional content.
4. **Blogging:** Start a niche blog and monetize through ads or affiliate marketing.
5. **Podcasting:** Launch a podcast on a topic you're passionate about.
6. **YouTube Channel:** Create content on a specific theme or interest.
7. **Self-Publishing:** Write and publish eBooks or guides.

8. **Music Production:** Produce music for artists, ads, or digital content.
9. **Art Commissions:** Create custom art pieces on commission.
10. **Digital Art Store:** Sell digital art prints or designs online.

TECHNOLOGY & SOFTWARE

11. **App Development**: Create apps for education, productivity, or entertainment.
12. **Website Design:** Offer web design services for small businesses and startups.
13. **Social Media Consulting:** Help brands optimize their social media presence.
14. **SEO Services:** Provide search engine optimization services to increase website visibility.
15. **Virtual Event Planning:** Organize and manage online events and conferences.
16. **E-commerce Solutions:** Develop and manage online stores for businesses.
17. **Tech Support Services:** Offer technical support for software and hardware issues.
18. **Mobile Game Development:** Design and publish mobile games.
19. **Cybersecurity Consulting:** Help businesses protect their data and online assets.
20. **Cloud Storage Solutions:** Offer secure cloud storage options.

RETAIL & E-COMMERCE

21. **Dropshipping:** Sell products online without holding inventory.
22. **Handmade Goods:** Sell handmade crafts, jewelry or art.
23. **Print-on-Demand:** Offer custom-designed apparel and accessories.
24. **Sustainable Products Store:** Sell eco-friendly and sustainable goods.
25. **Vintage Clothing:** Curate and sell vintage clothing online.

26. **Subscription Boxes:** Create and sell subscription boxes in a niche market.
27. **Tech Accessories:** Sell trendy tech accessories.
28. **Health and Wellness Products:** Offer health supplements and wellness products.
29. **Pet Supplies:** Sell pet food, toys, and accessories.
30. **Beauty and Personal Care:** Offer organic and cruelty-free beauty products.

FOOD & BEVERAGE

31. **Meal Prep Service:** Provide weekly prepared meal services.
32. **Bakery:** Start an online bakery with delivery options.
33. **Food Truck:** Operate a food truck with unique offerings.
34. **Healthy Snack Boxes:** Sell subscription boxes of healthy snacks.
35. **Catering Service:** Offer catering for small events or parties.
36. **Specialty Foods:** Produce and sell specialty foods like hot sauce or gourmet popcorn.
37. **Coffee Shop:** Open a small, local coffee shop with unique blends.
38. **Farmers Market Vendor:** Sell homemade or homegrown products at local markets.
39. **Craft Beverage Production:** Brew and sell craft beers, wines, or spirits.
40. **Nutrition Coaching:** Provide personalized nutrition plans and coaching.

SERVICES

41. **Personal Shopping:** Offer personal shopping services or style consulting.
42. **Cleaning Service:** Start a residential or commercial cleaning service.
43. **Laundry Service:** Provide laundry pickup and delivery services.
44. **Pet Sitting:** Offer pet sitting and dog walking services.
45. **Landscaping:** Provide landscaping and garden maintenance services.

46. **Handyman Services:** Offer repair and maintenance services for homes.
47. **Event Planning:** Plan and organize events or parties.
48. **Delivery Services:** Start a local delivery service for groceries or meals.
49. **Virtual Assistance:** Offer administrative and support services remotely.
50. **Car Wash and Detailing:** Provide mobile car washing and detailing services.

SUSTAINABLE & GREEN BUSINESSES

51. **Recycling Service:** Start a niche recycling service (e.g., electronics, plastics).
52. **Sustainable Fashion:** Create and sell eco-friendly and sustainable clothing.
53. **Green Consulting:** Offer consulting services to businesses aiming to become more sustainable.
54. **Eco-Friendly Packaging:** Design and sell biodegradable and eco-friendly packaging.
55. **Renewable Energy Projects:** Develop small-scale renewable energy solutions.
56. **Urban Gardening Solutions:** Offer products and services for city dwellers to grow their own food.
57. **Eco-Tourism:** Plan and organize eco-friendly tours and travel experiences.
58. **Sustainable Beauty Products:** Create and sell organic, cruelty-free beauty products.
59. **Green Cleaning Products:** Produce and distribute environmentally friendly cleaning supplies.
60. **Bicycle Repair and Rental:** Offer bicycle repair services and rentals for eco-friendly transportation.

PROFESSIONAL & FINANCIAL SERVICES

61. **Resume Writing Services:** Offer professional resume writing and editing services.
62. **Financial Advising for Students:** Provide financial planning services tailored for students.
63. **Market Research:** Conduct market research for small businesses.

64. **Freelance Writing:** Provide writing services for businesses and individuals.
65. **Legal Consulting:** Offer legal consulting services for startups or small businesses.
66. **Accounting Services:** Provide bookkeeping and accounting services.
67. **Real Estate Photography:** Specialize in photography for real estate listings.
68. **Translation Services:** Offer translation services for businesses or legal documents.
69. **IT Consulting:** Provide consulting services on IT infrastructure and software solutions.
70. **Procurement Services:** Provide procurement services to other businesses on products and services they need.

ENTERTAINMENT & LEISURE

71. **Event Ticket Resale:** Buy and resell tickets for popular events.
72. **Travel Planning:** Offer bespoke travel itinerary planning services.
73. **Sports Coaching:** Provide coaching services for specific sports.
74. **Board Game Café:** Open a café that offers food and board games.
75. **Adventure Sports:** Organize adventure sports outings like hiking, kayaking, or rock climbing.
76. **Book Club Subscription:** Start a subscription service for book enthusiasts.
77. **Virtual Reality Experiences:** Develop or offer virtual reality experiences and games.
78. **Hobby Classes:** Conduct classes for hobbies like knitting, pottery, or woodworking.
79. **Personalized Gift Service:** Create and sell personalized gifts.
80. **Escape Rooms:** Design and operate physical or virtual escape room experiences.

EDUCATION & TRAINING

81. **Online Tutoring:** Teach subjects you're proficient in.

82. **Language Teaching:** Offer classes in a second language.
83. **Educational Content Creation:** Develop and sell educational materials and courses.
84. **Skill Workshops:** Conduct workshops on valuable skills like coding, photography, etc.
85. **Career Coaching:** Assist individuals with resume building and interview preparation.
86. **Music Lessons:** Teach instruments or vocals online.
87. **Art Classes:** Host virtual art classes for various skill levels.
88. **Fitness Coaching:** Offer online fitness and wellness coaching.
89. **Technology Workshops:** Teach older adults how to use technology.
90. **Test Prep Services:** Provide preparation courses for standardized tests.

HEALTH & WELLNESS

91. **Yoga Instructor:** Offer online or in-person yoga classes.
92. **Personal Trainer:** Provide personalized fitness programs.
93. **Nutritional Supplements:** Sell health and nutritional supplements online.
94. **Meditation Workshops:** Conduct meditation sessions or workshops.
95. **Wellness Retreats:** Organize wellness retreats in nature-rich locations.
96. **Health Coaching:** Offer health and wellness coaching services.
97. **Telehealth Services:** Develop a platform for online medical consultations.
98. **Fitness Equipment Rental:** Rent out fitness equipment to individuals or gyms.
99. **Ergonomic Products:** Sell ergonomic furniture and accessories for home offices.
100. **Mental Health Counselling:** Provide online counselling and therapy services.

STEP 3

VALIDATE YOUR BUSINESS IDEAS

ENSURE YOUR BUSINESS IDEA WILL SELL BEFORE YOU START

Let's face the fact. Your business will only succeed if your potential clients buy into your idea. In other words, your business idea is only good to the extent at which your customers accept it. If you clients believe your product is bad, your business is as good as dead. If the same client believes your product is excellent, your business will flourish. This brings us to my most important rule when it comes to business ideas.

"Do not implement new business ideas immediately. Validate your ideas first"

This should serve as your golden rule for starting new businesses. Ideas almost always seem impeccable until you actually begin to implement. Product look nice until your customer begins to use them. Services seems like viable business proposition until client refuse to pay for it. Any business idea you generate will always seem marketable until you start showing it to potential clients. The feedback you receive from such potential client is what you will need to transform your idea into a business or improve the idea into a better business

6 WAYS TO VALIDATE YOUR BUSINESS IDEAS

So, you have finally come up with an excellent business idea and want to start your business immediately. You want to know whether there is market for your idea or not. The five step business ideas validation process will help you put your business idea to the test and decide whether there will be adequate demand for your product once you launch.

START WITH A SIMPLE SEARCH ONLINE: You have arrived at this awesome idea that will make you millions. In your mind this is the best business idea ever. But wait a minute! Your first step to validate your idea is to do a simple search to see if there is any other business operating the same model. So let assume you want to operate a fruit juice shop that will serve freshly squeezed fruit juice in your neighborhood. You figured you could expand that business and eventually supply the big supermarkets in your region. You Google your business idea and whoa!! There are over twenty businesses that are producing the same fruit squeeze and serving the same market you are targeting in your region. If this is you then there is good news. Coming by competitors already serving the same product in your market means there is demand for the product you want to sell. This Is good news. Next, ask yourself these simple questions: Can you add value to the existing product already being sold on the market? Will the market be willing to accept a more quality product than is currently being offered? If the answer is yes then you are on to something. Let move on to the next step

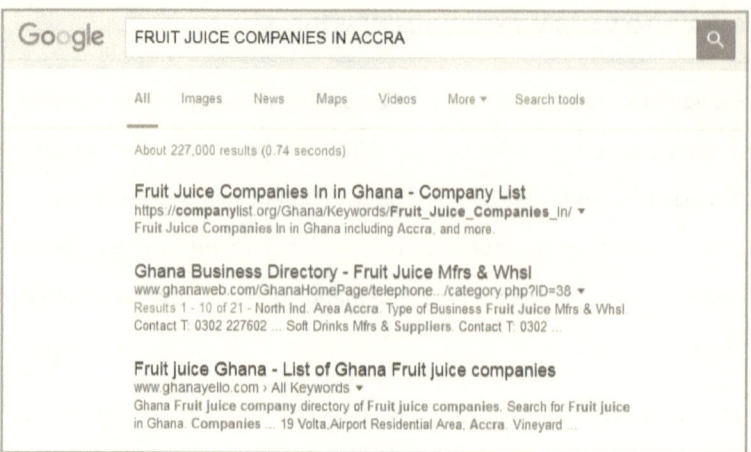

If your search returns just a handful of companies selling the same product, it may be an indication of how difficult it is for companies to generate revenue doing same business. These tend to deter people from offering the same product and should cause you to tread cautiously with your new idea.

SPEAK TO POTENTIAL CUSTOMERS: Having passed our first test, we are now ready to go through the next stage of our idea validation process for our fruit squeeze business idea. We want to know what others think about our idea and if they will be willing to buy your product should you start operation. Select 5 key people you trust and engage them for feedback on your business idea. Now assume we have settled on the 5 people you want to engage on our new business idea, you now present sample of your fruit juice to these potential customers and ask for their feedback. Try and get as much information about your product and how it compares to other products as possible. If possible, add samples of your competitor's product and let your 5 potential customers do an assessment of these products as well. For our Fruit juice business, we will be interested in answering the questions below

> **VALIDATION QUESTIONS TO ASK ABOUT YOUR PRODUCT**
> - What do you like about my product/service (Fruit Juice in this instance)?
> - What do you dislike about my product/service (Fruit Juice)?
> - How can I make my product better/how can I improve my product/service (Fruit Juice)?
> - Will you be willing to buy my product/service?
> - Why will you be willing to buy my products/service?
> - At what price will you be willing to buy my product/service (Fruit Juice)?

> **VALIDATION QUESTIONS TO ASK ABOUT YOUR COMPETITOR'S PRODUCT**
> - What do you like about this product/service (A Competitor's Fruit Juice in this instance)?
> - What do you dislike about this product/service?
> - What should be done to improve this product/service?
> - Is there any special reason why you will prefer this product (Fruit Juice) instead of my product/services?

Going through these questions with your potential client will let you know what factors drive sales and profitability in your chosen line of business. You will also have valuable information on how you can improve your product and make it more acceptable to your potential client. Use this information to improve your product and build an MVP (Minimum Viable Product) which you can show to your potential clients. After completing this stage, you are ready to proceed to our next stage.

BUILD A LANDING PAGE FOR YOUR IDEA: Up to this staged you have received real feedback from potential clients about your product. You have also used some of this feedback to learn the weakness in your competitor's product and how you can make our product better. You have used these two sets of information to improve your products and make it more marketable to your potential clients. Your next phase is to move a step higher and test if there is a wider market for our product. You can do this by creating a landing page for your business.

A landing page is just a one-page site your potential clients can visit if interested in your product. This usually appears when the potential client clicks on an online add, a social media page, an online search result or a promotional email. To be effective, you must set your landing page as if your business actually exists. This is to measure the interest from potential client and the market response should launch your products. Once you have succeeded in setting up your landing page, Create social media account on all major social media platform for your business in order to drive traffic to your new page. Let assume our fruit juice company would be called Nkwa Natural Fruit Juice (Nkwa is an Akan word that means Life). For students or young entrepreneur on a budget, try setting up your landing page using any of the free hosting services available. You should also understand most hosting services may display ads on your page or place some form of limitation on how you operate your account. You should read and understand what you are giving away when taking such free hosting services. Better still, there are a free hosting provider that provides hosting services free of ads. ByeHost.com, Wix.com and Yola.com are such a few of these services.

Once you have successfully set up your landing page, you will begin to get feedback and also gather contact that could end up becoming your real clients when you finally start your business. Use the response you receive from the landing page to gauge whether there is enough support for your business. Once you are convinced your idea is good to go, you are on to something.

USE AD TOOL FROM FACEBOOK TO ESTIMATE POTENTIAL MARKET SIZE: One of the most effective ways to gauge the market size of your idea is through Facebook ad tool. Its effectiveness lies in its ability to target specific demographic and social group. If you sell ladies cloth, you can target all ladies within specific age group from your country, region or even city. By specifying the demographic, interests, behavior and other details, Facebook then estimate the potential market size according the interest you have chosen. To use Facebook ad tool, navigate your browser to www.facebook.com/ads/manager/creation after you have logged into your Facebook account. When you navigate to the page for the first time, the return page will look like figure 1.3 below.

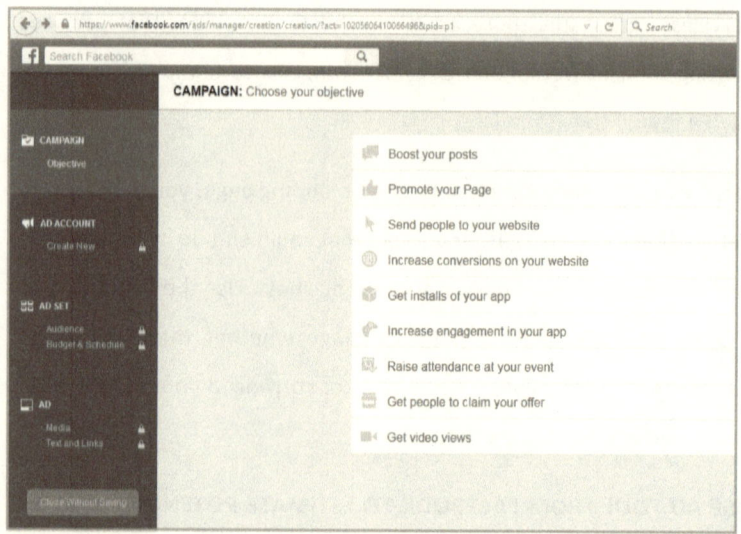

FIGURE 1.3: FACEBOOK AD MANAGER

Choose any of the campaigns listed and enter your geographical location, interests, behaviors and any other details you wish to query. For estimating the potential market size of our fruit juice business, we are interested in both male and female from Greater Accra in Ghana whose interest includes Juice, Pineapple Juice, Orange Juice, Simply Orange and Simply Lemonade. This exercise should last for about 10 minutes and comes at no cost. And since one can say pretty much everyone is on Facebook these days, it means our answer will be fairly accurate representation of our potential market size.

Now back to our fruit juice business. For male and Female of 15-50 years with interest in Juice, Pineapple Juice, Orange Juice, Simply Orange and Simply Lemonade, Facebook estimates the market size to be 38,000.00 (FIGURE 3.4). This over 38,000 people in Greater Accra alone who likes or are interested in Fruit Juice. There is certainly a market for our chosen business.

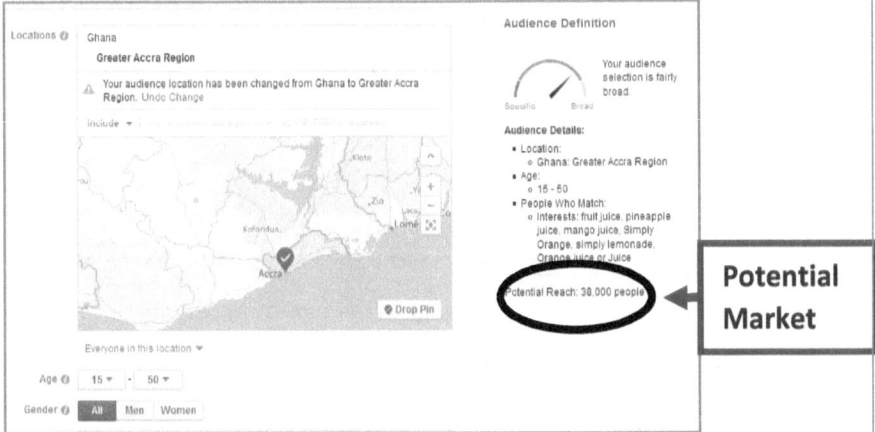

As an entrepreneur, you must learn to gather information and use resources around you to make informed decisions. Validating your business idea will help you refine and business your product/services and better serve your target market.

STEP 4

DEVELOP CORE SKILLS

YOU WILL BE MOST SUCCESSFUL FOCUSING ON YOUR AREA OF STRENGTH

Of all students' entrepreneurs, Bill Gates stands out as one of the early pioneers of modern computing. Whiles he is not the first person to neither invent the computer nor develop software for that matter, his contribution and inventions revolutionized and transformed the computing industry into what it's become today.

DEVELOPING KEY SKILLS IN COMPUTING

Bill Gates wasn't born into an engineering or computing family that will offer family support. His father was a lawyer and his mother a teacher. His parent had originally wanted the young Bill Gates to grow up to become a lawyer. At the age of 13, Gates was enrolled at Lakeside School, where he first saw a computer, developed an interest in computing and began to program in BASIC. The School bought one computer and a Teletype which it allowed student to pay and use. The School had also bought time for its students at General Electric where they get to use the company's computers. Gates developed a keen interest in learning to program and was constantly excused by the school to enable him advanced his interest in programming. When the school started limiting the time students could spend using the computer, Gates hacked into the school computer to allow him more time on the computer. The school discovered this and banned Gates from using the computer. The school later rescinded its decision when it realized Gates has develop core skills in programming, deciding instead to allow Gates to use the computer in exchange for which he will help them fix bugs on the computer.

Bill Gates wrote his first computer program using the school's computer. It was called Tic-Tac-Toe and allowed users to play games against the computer. After Gates money was exhausted, he sought to use another computer belonging to a company called Computer Centre Corporation (CCC). Gates spent time studying various source codes for the programs that runs on the computer until 1970 when the company collapsed. Next, he teamed up with four other students including his longtime friend Paul Allen to write a computer program for his school to assign students to their classes.

NOT YOUR AVERAGE STUDENT: For all his interest in programming, Bill Gates was more than what you will call your average student. He scored 1590 out of 1,600 on SAT and gained admission to Harvard in 1973. It was at Harvard that Bill Gates finally set out on the road to becoming one of the most celebrated tech entrepreneurs the world has ever seen.

At Harvard, Gates co-authored a paper on the topic "Bound for Sorting by Prefix Reversal" with his college professor Prof. Christos Papadimitriou. The paper Gates co-authored was on a decade old problem called 'pancake sorting'. According to his math professor, Gates was the most serious and intelligent students of any students his age. He had discovered how to solve the decade old mathematical puzzle of "pancake sorting" by $1.67n$ flips at the time when the world thought you could only do so with $2n$ flips. It will take another 30 years before this record will be surpassed.

THE FOUNDING OF MICROSOFT: Gates interest in mathematics and passion for computing will lead to a strong desire in computing and development of microchip processors. Gates will then leave Harvard to pioneer the development of the microchip processor that will revolutionize computing and trigger a wave of innovation that will transform our manufacturing-based economies to that of information-based economy. It was in January, 1975 that Gates read an article in a magazine about a new computer called Altair 8800. Gate contacted the manufacturers and informed them he has developed new software that could be installed on their Altair 8800 computer. Gates did this purely to gauge the interest of the manufacturers as they had not written any program that could run on the Altair 8800 at that time. Realizing that the company will be interested; gates immediately set to work that night to develop a software that could run on the Altair 8800. The company took an interest in their software and hired Gates longtime friend Allen, while Gates took a leave of absence from Harvard to enable them complete their project. Gates and Allen called their new company Microsoft.

Microsoft quickly emerged as a leading tech company with their operation system Microsoft Windows leading the way in visual based programming. Gates was a visionary, and imagined a world where every home will have a computer running Microsoft Windows. He patented his software and with the help of his father who was a lawyer, ensured that other companies or programmers did not copy their software without payment. By the time he turned 39 years, Bill Gates had become the richest man in the world, a position he will maintain for several years.

ACQUIRE RELEVANT KNOWLEDGE, DEVELOP CORE SKILLS

Gates meteoric rise can largely be attributed to developing key competences and skills in computing among others reasons. Every student entrepreneur must lay this solid foundation in order to succeed. It is not merely `enough to have an Idea about what you want to do, but also imperative to develop professional grade skills in your chosen field. For students' entrepreneurs, my advice is simple

"Acquire relevant knowledge, develop core skills"

Finding yourself in a study environment present you with advantages that will not be available to the ordinary entrepreneur. Your world revolves around an institution of learning purposely established to make sure student like you are imbibed with key knowledge and skills to be able to succeed in the real world. Like Bill Gates, you must make the most of your school and acquire relevant knowledge and skills you will need to succeed as an entrepreneur.

WHAT KIND OF SKILLS DO YOU NEED TO SUCCEED AS AN ENTREPRENEUR?

The advent of the information age brought with it, new demands for every entrepreneur. No matter the kind of business you will like to start, you will still need these key skills in order to make it in the world of business. The first skills I will discuss have become so indispensable even existing and already established businesses that do not embrace it end up failing. In all, I will discuss 10 KEY SKILLS which are a requirement for every aspiring entrepreneur. These skills can be learnt, developed or acquired so never doubt your potential in any way.

LEADERSHIP: Starting your own business comes with the responsibility of working with people to achieve your goals. Employees will join your company who will contribute their quota to your business but will ultimately look up to you for direction and motivation. Partners and financiers will back you based on your conviction and ability to articulate your vision and goals. All of these people have a role to play in your business, but the ultimate responsibility rest on you as the founder and originator of the business. You should show clear leadership, focus and rise above conflicts, setback and lead your team to achieve the goal you have set for your business. This is your sole responsibility an entrepreneur.

TECH SKILLS: One key characteristics of the modern age economy (or information age) is the migration of business from community based to online based. As the world get more computerized and mobile, more and more people are switching to doing business online. This has implication for entrepreneurs who do not migrate their businesses online. It means your company will lose business as more and more people migrate their purchases online. Developing your skills in tech is the first advice I give any student entrepreneur or startup. Let start with the basic of what you need to know in tech as startup entrepreneur.

SOCIAL MEDIA: Social media have assumed a market status in business. It is no longer a place for just sharing pictures and speaking your mind. If you are an entrepreneur, it is important you know how to market your brand and push your sales through social media. The easy platforms that come to mind are Facebook, X (formerly Twitter), Instagram, LinkedIn and YouTube. You must work on multiple platforms and know the basic of what social media marketing.

BASIC HTML AND WORDPRESS: Ok, you don't have to be an expert web developer or coder, but having a good understanding of how html works and being able to code in basic html will greatly enhance your understanding of how you can use the worldwide web to sell your business. It is also important to understand that as a young entrepreneur, you may not have the capital to fund a fully managed website which means being able to create simply website yourself will be much helpful in this regard.

WORDPRESS: WordPress is a web content management system. It was originally created as a tool to publish blogs but has evolved to support publishing other web content, including more traditional websites, mailing lists and Internet forum, media galleries, membership sites etc. Every student entrepreneur must learn to work with WordPress which provides a platform to design ecommerce and general website without having coding knowledge.

EMAIL MARKETING: You must learn to maintain regular contacts with clients with basic email marketing. Regularly share new products update and constantly inform clients of the benefit of doing business with you. This is different from spamming your clients with unnecessary emails. If possible, allow each client you serve to subscribe to an email service where you share relevant information on your business, products and services.

SEARCH ENGINE OPTIMISATION (SEO): When potential clients search any of your products or services being sold by your business, does your company's name appear in the search results? If not, you are losing out on business. As an entrepreneur it is important to have basic insight in search engine optimization (SEO) and how you can use it to drive your business. Again, your web developer can advise you and render such services for a fee. But you will save money knowing how to drives business online yourself if you acquire such knowledge.

SALES: All successful entrepreneurs know how to convince the world to buy into their products and services. If you want your startup to survive, I suggest you make selling skills a priority. As an entrepreneur, every action you take will revolve around sales. You will have to sell to your clients, sponsors, partners, bankers, investors, suppliers, even employees. You will need to convince a lot of people to buy into your business in order to be successful. Most importantly, learn to make relationship selling a core attribute of your new business at the early stage of your business.

Relationship selling simply means developing and deepening a long-term relationship with you clients. Instead of viewing a purchase a one-time transaction, relationship selling demands that you see a purchase as a start of a business relationship. This allows you to generate repeat business and referrals from your clients which will enables your business to grow.

RESILIENCE AND PERSISTENCE: This is one of the most important skills you should develop as an entrepreneur. Resilience or persistence simply refer to your ability to withstand disappointment, rejection or failure in your business and not give up on your goal. Every entrepreneur that has succeeded has had to overcome some form of disappointments or setbacks.

ANALYSE RISK AND MANAGE RISK: Entrepreneurs are risk takers. They embrace risk when others ovoid such risks. They also understand and manages risk better which is what you must learn in order to become a better entrepreneur.

FOCUS: Managing a successful enterprise demand long term focus that will allow you steer your business in the direction you have planned and envisioned for your business. A successful entrepreneur focuses on growing his business in the long term and aligning short term decision to long term goals.

PEOPLE SKILLS: Great businesses are built with great team. Your business will only succeed when you attract the right kind of employees that will contribute to your vision and productivity. This is very vital especially at the early stage of your business. The people you employ at this stage must add real value to your team and should make significant contribution to help you advance your business' interest. You must learn how to motivate your team and articulate a clear vision that will synchronize your actions and cause you to focus your actions on achieving your visions together. The foundation you lay with people will determine the kind of results your new business will achieve in the future.

CURIOSITY: The world of business is constantly changing, which demand that entrepreneurs must learn to embrace new ideas and constantly improve on their processes. As an entrepreneur, you must question everything around you and constantly ask how it can be improved. You must develop a mind that generate, evaluates and think about new ideas every day and every time. You should also be a lifetime learner and constantly strive on acquiring relevant knowledge that feeds your business with innovation. This is what makes entrepreneurs successful in the information age.

TIME MAGEMENT SKILL: As a student entrepreneur, you will be combining studies with businesses which will require you make efficient use of your time to avoid burnout and exhaustion along the way. You must be able to plan your day and allocate the right amount of time to manage your business whiles learning and attending lectures at the same time. This is one of the most important skills I advise students to develop even before they decide to become entrepreneurs. A successful entrepreneur must learn to manage and save time through multitasking, priority setting, delegation and operating by deadlines.

UNDERSTAND FINANCIAL STATEMENTS: The world of business has its own language which you must learn if you want to be successful as an entrepreneur, it is called financial statements. Every young entrepreneur should be able to understand financial statement and learn basic bookkeeping in order to make successful pitches especially to financiers and backers who will be much interested in how you demonstrate a solid understanding of your business before backing you with their money. As your business expands, you will be able to hire professional accountants who will absolve these functions and perform these roles fulltime. Knowing how to analyze business statements will however help you make better judgment and decision even if you have a fulltime accountant and should be encouraged.

STEP 5

CREATE PARTNERSHIP

THE SINGLE MOST IMPORTANT DETERMINANT OF YOUR SUCCESS ARE WHO YOU START WITH

No one will doubt Warren Buffet is among the greatest entrepreneurs alive today. The oracle of Omaha as he has come to be called is currently chairman of Berkshire Hathaway. Buffet, who started as a student entrepreneur, is now worth $135 billion (as at March 2024) whiles his company, Berkshire Hathaway has asset of $948.5 billion with annual revenue of $$302.1B billion as at Dec. 2023.

As his worth has rocketed, so has his reputation. Warren Buffet has become one of the most coveted entrepreneurs in the world today, with entrepreneurs and business leaders all over the world paying millions to have a one-on-one time with him. Buffet, who is also an ardent philanthropist, started auctioning a 'power lunch' since 2000 at a charity event for GLIDE Foundation, a non-for-profit organization that supports the poor and marginalized. Business leaders from all over the world bid for lunch with Buffet. The successful bid gets to have exclusive lunch with buffet together with 7 other friends at which they are allowed to ask him any question they want. In 2014, Singapore businessman Andy Chua paid and amount of $2.2 million for a lunch date with Warren Buffet. The highest amount ever paid for lunch with Buffet was in the year 2022 when a record amount of $19 million was paid by an anonymous bidder.

In 2007, Mohnish Pabrai, Managing Partner of Pabrai Investments paid an amount of $650,000.00 to have lunch with Buffet. After more than three hours of spending time with the acclaimed entrepreneur, Pabrai stated that the biggest lesson he learned from having a three-hour chat with Warren Buffet was the value of creating the right relationship or partnership. Pabrai said meeting Warren Buffet was an opportunity to learn from one of the greatest business minds of his time. He wanted to understand what philosophy and values has made Buffet so successful, and meeting Warren Buffet made him change his life a major way:

> "The lunch made me realize that I had constantly undervalued the power of making sure I am constantly around people who are better than me, and around whom I can improve".

After time with Warren Buffet, Pabrai began to pay more attention to the kind of relationship and partnership he creates and the people he hangs out with. Businesses are built through beneficial relationships, partnerships and alliances. You must learn to establish an enduring and longer termed relationship with the right clients and business partners in order to create value for your business.

For student and young entrepreneurs aiming to succeed in business, forming the right partnership and relationships can mean the difference between failing and succeeding and such a decision should be made only after thoughtful thinking and careful considerations. Partnership can help you team up with people that will make valuable contribution to your business and support your startup to create value at its early stages.

SUCCESSFUL ENTREPRENEURS FORM THE RIGHT PARTNERSHIP

Let come back to our Fruit Juice Business. So, we have this amazing business idea to start a fruit juice business and distribute our juice to all major supermarkets in Accra, Ghana. I have discussed the idea with few people and have also validated it to know if there is a potential market for my product. I am convinced there is a market for my fruit juice and I will able to sell if I start production. I am arranging to buy some fruits from the local market so I can start selling to the immediate shops around my school.

But what if the ideas I have in my mind won't work out as I have anticipated? Who will present a counter opinion and make suggestions on how we can improve on my initial idea? What if the shops around my school refuse to sell my fruit juice after I start production? Who will go to the market and buy the raw materials? Who will distribute the fresh juice and follow up for payments? How do I promote the new product am I about to sell? Do I have to put up all the startup capital alone? Do I have to do all these alone or should I have a partner?

Successful entrepreneurs all over the world have recognized and embraced the benefits of forming partnership and creating beneficial relationship to advance their business. And this ran through every successful entrepreneur I have had an encounter with. Even where the decision is to go solo without any partnership, success will to a large extend depend on having reliable, trustworthy and dependable staff, clients, suppliers, mentors or financiers that commit themselves like partners to your new business. In reality, whether your go solo or you form partnership, you will still be dependent on some form of support or help from staff, investors, clients, friends or family, and the depth of this relationship will be a major factor that will determine what you are able to achieve as an entrepreneur.

There is an inspiring story of how Databank started in in Ghana with only three young professional who returned to Ghana in the 1980s with the goal of starting an investment bank at a time when many people did not even understand what investing was. Ken Ofori-Atta, Keli Gadzekpo and James Akpo formed the triad-partnership that dreamed and nurtured the idea of starting an investment bank which is now Databank today. The three partners finally set up their first office at Kantamanto with a loan they accessed in 1990 with initial focus on business and financial research and compilation of data to support financial and capital market. From that small office, Databank established a niche as market leaders in business and financial market research across Africa. The company has now expanded with regional subsidiaries across Africa. The company also manages Africa's leading mutual fund (the EPACK) which has significant investments in Ghana, Mauritius, South Africa, Morocco, Nigeria, Uganda, Tanzania, Egypt, Zambia and Malawi. Databank also manages Ghana's first ever money market fund (the MFUND) as well as the Databank Balanced Fund which collectively totals in excess of GH¢ 200 million.

One key factor that accounted for the early success of the Databank was the triad partnership of Ken, Keli and James: Ken Ofori-Atta and Keli Gadzakpo were both finance and accounting professional working in US. Ken at Wall Street whiles Keli was working with KPMG in Washington. James Akpo (who later became HRM Togbe Afede) had just graduated with MBA from Yale University. The three partners brought the right mix of knowledge, skills, experience, passion and enthusiasm that was a leading factor in the success of databank.

You will find the story of partnership that accounted for databank success is a common denominator in many successful startups all over the world. Bill Gates, one of the most successful student entrepreneurs started Microsoft with his childhood friend and partner Paul Allen. Steve Jobs started Apple Inc. with Steve Wozniak. Bill Hewlett started hp (Hewlett Packard) with Dave Packard and Albert Ocran started Combert Impressions with Comfort Ocran. Successful entrepreneurs know the values of creating the right relationship and they create these relationships at the start of their business to help them achieve success.

THE 10 KEY QUESTIONS TO ASK WHEN FORMING PARTNERSHIP

If you are thinking of forming a partnership for your business, it is important to answer the following 10 question to enable you make an informed decision. Partnership can create value and benefit for your startup, as well as conflict and disagreements.

IS THERE A REAL NEED? Alliances and partnership are forged to grow businesses. They bring a lot of advantages and real benefits until the partnership goes bad and disagreements begin to appear. Conflict may arise about how sales should be conducted, how profits should be shared, whether or how additional staff should be employed, whether partners should be paid for their role and who is responsible for what role.

As a young entrepreneur, starting your own business comes with tremendous stress and responsibilities. It is no mean an easy road to be taken lightly. Having a partner you can count on can remove some of this burden and ensure you have a second opinion to help you make or think through difficult decisions. If there is a real need and benefit you can derive from bringing a partner on board, then am all for it. But before you make a decision, you should identify very tangible benefit you can derive from such partnership. If you can't identify any real benefit your new partner will bring to your business, then it is better to go solo.

IS THERE COMMITMENT? You are passionate about your new business and believe your passion and dedication will pay off later. It is important to see that level of commitment in your partner too. Startup requires strenuous commitments and input at their infant stages which means any partner must be committed to the new business for the partnership to yield any desired result.

WHAT KEY STRENGTH DO THEY BRING? Partnerships are productive when each partner brings key skills and strength to the business. You partners should add value from having knowledge, skills or network that can benefit your business in a major way. They should have a key value proposition that you lack and should strengthen the business with their presence. Having key experience with a successful competitor can help. Having connection and network that can benefit the business can help, and abilities to make pitch and sales are certainly a plus.

RESPONSIBILITY ASSIGNMENT: Closely tied to the idea of choosing a partner with key strength or skill is the idea of letting the partner understand in clear and unambiguous terms what role they will be expected to play in the new business. This is also tied to the idea of having a clear need for a partner before entering into any partnership. Your partner should be assigned a specific role and this should be discussed to enable him/her understand your expectation and the role he/she will be expected to play in the new business.

ARE THEY WILLING TO COMMIT TIME TO THE BUSINESS? Startups require time and effort especially at the initial stages. This is especially so when there is no paid staff and the founders must devote time and energy to every task and responsibilities the new business may require. Any partner that joins must be willing to devote adequate time to any job role he is assigned to. Without such commitments, it becomes impossible to achieve sales and other targets for the new business. It is important to discuss and find out what time and commitment your potential partner is willing to sacrifice before any decision is made.

(INVESTMENT CONTRIBUTION) HOW MUCH ARE THEY CONTIRBUTING TO THE BUSINESS? Partners are going to have a stake in your business and will have a share in any future profit or value that will be created. They should show commitment and be willing to contribute both financially and materially to the new business. Will each partner be required to make a specific financial contribution? Is any partner bringing a major asset or machinery to the new business? Are you willing to accept sweat equity if a partner is not in a position to make financial contribution? The details of such contributions can vary from startup to startup, but usually depends on how the partnership is setup. It is important such discussion is made prior to any commitment and each partner is clear on what he/she must contribute towards setting up the new business.

(HONESTY CAPITAL) ARE THEY TRUSTWORTHY? For all the benefit a partnership can bring, there is always the possibility of a partner overstating their credentials in order have more stake or shares in the business. For this reason, it is important to know partners are really who they say they are and can make the kind of contribution for which you want to partner them in your new business. If you want a partner that can help you sell your products, try letting him make sales or confirming if he has the network and contact to be able to succeed in sales. You should also understand how a person stay committed to his words will determine how suppliers and financiers will support your new business. Honesty is social capital in business. You can use it to buy goods and transact business same way as you use money. Some of the most successful entrepreneurs I have worked with have suppliers and backers who are willing to finance large project simply because of the trust they have earned being honest on much smaller projects. If you can't find your new partner to be trustworthy now, my advice is not to enter into any partnership for now.

ARE THEY WILLING TO WORK WITHOUT PAY? As a student entrepreneur, you may have to spent lot of time building your client base before being able to reward yourself with a decent wage. In the same manner your new business may not be able to afford paying competitive wages and may require that partners put in extra time and take up additional responsibility in order to ensure low staff cost. Even where additional staff is paid competitive wages, founders and partners may still have to work without competitive wage. It is important your partner understand the cash situation of your new business before they make a decision to join the business. This will likely prevent future conflict and also help you to operate your business at a low cost until your startup has an adequate footing to start paying competitive wages.

EXPENSE AND PROFIT DISTRIBUTION: What if the new business runs out of cash and the partners have to put forward new rounds of capital. Again, how should major expense be distributed among partners? How do you finance a large order and who is responsible for which expense? You should also discuss how profits are to be shared and what proportion of profits should be retained and reinvested into growing the business.

(EXIT STRATEGY) HOW WILL YOU HANDLE A SPLIT? Let face the truth; not all partnership will work out, and this should not necessarily mean the end of your business. Before you enter into any partnership, it is important to discuss what happens when a partner decides he/she is no longer interested in the business. How do you handle a partner that wants to be bought out of the business? What happens if one of the partners dies? Discussing these prior to forming business partnership can save you a lot of conflicts and even litigation in the future and should be discussed at the start of every business partnership.

ARE THEY WILLING TO COMMIT TO A WRITTEN AGREEMENT? One of the most important decisions to make regarding any partnership is whether your new partner is willing to sign a written agreement or contract on the partnership. This is a very important and necessary step to take and it clears a lot of misunderstanding, conflicts and spells out the rights and obligation of each partner in the new business. You should also understand that you can't hold new partners to their words without any written agreement which means they may consider any verbal assurance they give you as not legally binding until it is put out in writing. All the issues discussed such the obligation and role of each partner, the time each partner needs to spend on the new business, how a split should be management and how profit is to be shared should be spelt out in a written agreement. Even where the business is registered as partnership, having a separate written agreement that spell out the obligations and responsibilities from each partner will benefit the business and should always be done.

STEP 6

START SMALL – BEAT THE INEXPERIENCE BARRIER

HOW TO OVERCOME THE STUDENT ENTREPRENEUR GREATEST CHALLENGE

The year was 2006. I was in my final year of a BA Economics – Sociology course at KNUST and I had finally succeeded in putting one of my long-held business ideas into action. I called it the Business Development Foundation, a capacity building initiative to train and encourage other students to be entrepreneurial. It had taking me a whole year dreaming and planning this particular event and had saved enough money from my student's loan to be able to finally start.

From the start, I had put together the names of 5 prominent entrepreneurs and business leaders I intended to invite as resource persons to my event. I had worked on the event concepts and had further discussions with student societies to partner my events. A friend introduced me to a student worker who owed a printing press and was willing to print my posters and publicity materials for me on credit bases. It was the best arrangement I could ever make as it will free me from paying immediately, the cost of printing more than a 1000 poster for the event. I proceeded to make arrangement for the posters which went into print immediately. I had discussion with two other friends about partnering the event for which they readily agreed. After meeting them and explaining the event concept and ideas to them, they were of the opinion the ideas was good and they will partner me to organize the event.

Later that month I travelled to Accra to meet and invite the 5 speakers I had selected to speak at the event. I wrote officially to all the speakers inviting them to speak at the event anticipating I will receive their response in a fortnight, but response were short in coming. After a month, I had still not received any confirmation from my proposed speakers except two that has asked me to pay a fee of GHC500.00 respectively to enable them speaks at the event. I realized I had committed a grave error in not inviting the speakers on time and not following up immediately I submitted the invitation.

Worse, the printing press had gone ahead with the printing job and had completed the printing of 1000 posters using the names of the speakers I had proposed who had not yet confirmed. Third error! I had discussed credit terms with the printing press but had not asked for an official invoice detailing our agreement and the pricing. After printing the posters, the printing price gave me an invoice that was far in excess than what we officially agreed. It was a grave error that will cost more than 50% of the student loan I had saved towards financing my project. More administrative expense popped up which began to eat into the little saving I had made. I proceeded to select three more speakers for the event but that meant I will have to print new posters which will double the cost of printing which I wasn't prepared for. Worse still, my two other partners were not ready to invest in the project financially as we did not discuss extensively the details of the partnership and the financial contribution we had to make. To solve this problem, I spoke to three microfinance institutions about accessing loans for the project but none were willing to trust a student startup. One of the finance houses after listening to my extensive presentation decided they could support the project but will need a security which should be a vehicle that is less than 8 years. Obviously as a student entrepreneur I did not have the collateral they were requesting, and couldn't access the loan. Next, I spoke to a couple of relatives, and got my sister to give me a loan of a GHc1,000.00 while my dad also applied for a loan from a microfinance institution to support my project.

With the new injection of capital, I was able to pay the speakers that had agreed to come and also rent the venue for the event. We started publicizing the event a week prior to the event date. We have discussed with most student societies on campus and they were ready to support. We also ensured the posters were posted to every corner of the university and other educational institutions in the region. At this stage all seemed to be moving smoothly till the consequence of one grave error came knocking at my door. Two of the initial 5 speakers I had invited as resource persons for the events had eventually informed me, that they are unable to attend and were not pleased their names appeared on the event posters. They threatened to file a lawsuit and asked I issued a disclaimer on all major radio stations that their names appeared in error and are not speaking at the event.

That very night necessitated an urgent response. I made travelling arrangement at dawn and got to Accra to meet the two speakers and verbally apologize the next morning. I explained the circumstances that led to printing of the posters early and how I had made some initial mistakes as a student entrepreneur. After the apologies, I returned to Kumasi the same day and started preparing our team for the event the next day.

The workshop was a success. Even though I had made mistakes that had led to increased cost, the publicity had been good and had resulted in more than 1,500 students participating in the summit. Proceed from the summit were enough to cover cost which enabled us to repay the loans from relatives and other suppliers (including the printing press) immediately. After the workshop, I went on a thank you visit to the all resource person who spoke at the workshop. But there was one last task still to be done. I returned to the two speakers that did not speak at the workshop with official written apologies. One of these speakers is a regular speaker and has an event consulting company. After accepting my apology letter, I spent an eye opening 30 minutes discussing my workshop with him. That 30-minute taught me more lessons in event management than the entire year I spent organizing my own workshop. As I listened to him speak, I began to think about how I could have saved so much cost and avoided so many mistakes if I have had this conversation earlier.

This chapter is dedicated to helping student entrepreneurs overcome one of their greatest challenges – inexperience. It is important to minimize costly errors as a young entrepreneur and to exercise good judgment when taking business decisions.

SMALL BEGINNING ARE PRICELES

There is a reason most student business starts in student dormitories and parent garages, with very little or no capital. When you start with little investment, the costs of indecisions are less. But most importantly, the mindset and orientation of young entrepreneurs who are willing to start small gives them the greatest advantage.

Every entrepreneur needs two key orientations or believes to be successful. The first is that *the future can be better than the present*. This means regardless of where you start, your situation can improve with better result. The second mindset is that *you determine what your future will be*. It is the decision you take today, or refuse to take today that will determine whether the future will be better or worse. Young entrepreneurs must develop these two mindsets to be successful in business.

Small beginnings also bring another advantage most entrepreneurs overlook. At the early stage of your business, you should be much more concerned about achieving three broad objectives.

- The first is providing quality and innovative service that will be accepted by your target market
- The second is attracting and retaining quality clients
- And the third is expanding and growing your business revenue.

These three objectives should be the focus of every young entrepreneur. Your startup can succeed, but only if it is able to achieve these three broad objectives to a large extent. Most entrepreneurs that are willing to start small understand these and work hard to achieve the three objectives above.

Perhaps, the most important benefit I have discovered about starting small is in starting in itself. What I am referring at? People who want to start their business only after mobilizing a large startup capital don't really start at all. Businesses are seldom started from the position of comfort. Such people tend to defer their dream and never really start any business at all which is quite the opposite for entrepreneurs willing to start with whatever resource they have. These are the entrepreneurs that start table top business but ends up owning corporations ten or twenty years later. What you start with doesn't matter, what you believe (your mindset) you can achieve with your little resource is your greatest assets.

7 BEST STRATEGIES FOR BEATING THE INEXPERIENCE BARRIER

Nothing can be more disheartening than giving your best business pitch and being told second later that all your effort count for nothing because you are too young to be an entrepreneur. I experienced these multiple times when I started a business in school called the BHuD Group. In our part of the world (Africa to be specific), age has historically been equated to wisdom and knowledge for so long, which can explain why your youthful age can be a source of frustration if not handled properly. This negative challenge is however dwarfed by the endless number of young people that are starting and succeeding in their own business. Successful young entrepreneurs learn to quickly come out of the inexperience barrier by adopting the strategies below

EMBRACE TECHNOLOGY AND INNOVATION: More than any other factor, technology has contributed to the explosion in the number of successful startups we are witnessing all over the world from young entrepreneurs. Young people who are more likely to embrace new technology are driving a change in the global economy by constantly adopting information technology to tackle business problems which were inefficiently being solved by traditional business models.

In time past, entry into most business was pretty much difficult if not impossible for young adults. The first barrier was the financial cost of setting up offices, filling it with staff and producing and stocking up products/inventory you want to sell. These constraints were pretty much what were needed to prevent young people from entering into business. The advent of the internet has however become a game changer.

The internet has presented an equal playing field where the big companies and the small companies can have equal access to the world market. This has come at very little cost. You can set up a company that serves market in Afghanistan, Canada and Hong Kong in a student dormitory with no more than one or two staff and immediately start selling.

This has obviously accounted for the explosion in the number of young millionaires some of whom are in their twenties. There are sites such as under30ceo.com that is devoted sorely to helping and publishing about such young business/entrepreneurs. If you are young and want to start a business, exploring the internet is one of the best ways to start a new business.

HAVE A MENTOR: This is an absolute must have if you want to succeed as a young entrepreneur. A mentor is an experienced and successful business person/entrepreneur who has gained several years of experience and knowledge in business and is willing to advise and share knowledge with you to help your new business succeed. A good mentor is valuable assets that will help you avoid early mistakes and will push you to the boundary of success as an entrepreneur.

My experience with my event company as a student taught me the necessity for a mentor when starting out as a young inexperienced entrepreneur. This is necessary not only for young entrepreneurs alone as entrepreneurs that have been in business for a long time always have very important counsel they can refer to as a mentor. If you are starting out as a young entrepreneur, follow the guidelines to choose a mentor and ensure you make the most of your mentor-mentoree relationship.

BE BEST IN WHAT YOU DO: Most people who meet will respect you once they realize you are absolutely good and know what your business is about. As an entrepreneur, it is important to understand the fact that no one should know your business more than you do. You must understand how your business operates and what you require to succeed like the palm of your hands. Knowing and understand your business, market and ensuring you acquire the necessary technical knowledge to manage a successful business let most people appreciate young as a young entrepreneur.

One mistake most entrepreneurs do is the tendency to overlook and take for granted, aspect of their business with time. As time passes on, and as we are faced with the challenges of doing business in the real world, we tend to forget the mission and vision we set for ourselves at the beginning of the business. Our business plan become less relevant and we begin to drift further from the vision we had when starting the business.

No one should know your business better than you do. A good entrepreneur should be able to demonstrate a clear and solid understanding of his business and also be able to convince relevant stakeholders about the viability of his business. This usually involves demonstrating high understanding and expertise in your field of business, in addition to providing relevant financial projections to support the fact that your company has the potential to be a successful profit generating business whiles projecting stronger performance in the future. I have identified four key areas where you need to demonstrate clear understanding and expertise:

What are you into? (Field): You must demonstrate you have adequate knowledge to operate business in your field (sector) and you have acquired the right knowledge to be able to perform in your business. SinceE:\since you do not have the benefit of experience, you must understand that demonstrating good, relevant knowledge should be key to convincing any partner about your business' potential.

Whom do you sell to? (Market): You need to demonstrate a clear understanding of the factors that shape competition in your industry or field. Having adequate knowledge of your market and how best to generate sales convinces potential partners/investors that you can generate sufficient revenue to cover your cost and be profitable should they invest in your business. What factors affect price setting in your industry and what are the parameters that affect client decision to buy or not to buy in that market. Is the market for your products seasonal and which product is likely to sell more during which particular season? Answering this question confidently and demonstrating a clear understanding of your market will let potential investors or partners understand the nature of your business.

Where are you now? Most important to knowing your business is demonstrating a clear understanding of your current performance and where your business will be in the near future. What project are you currently working on, what resource will you need, and how soon can you supply should you receive orders from clients.

Where do you go from here? Next to knowing your business is being able to demonstrate a clear understanding of your vision and where your business will be in the future. What strategies have your put in place and how will these strategies impact on your performance. This should clearly tell your bank how you are likely to perform in the future.

HIRE EXPERIENCE/LEAVERAGE OTHER PEOPLE KNOWLEDGE: Your startup may be small and you may not be in a position to employ a lot of staff. But eventually you will get to a stage where you need to hire and this where experience should play a role. You must learn to leverage and operates on other people experience and knowledge aside what you bring to your new business. Entrepreneurship is all about leveraging other people resource and knowledge to achieve the vision for your business. Successful entrepreneurs don't necessarily have the best ideas. Neither are they the smartest people in the world. Most successful entrepreneurs have very good people skills that they use to motivate others to achieve the goals and plan they set for their business.

HAVE AN EXPERIENCED BOARD: All companies limited by shares are required to have a Board of Directors that supervise governance. Board of Directors plays a major role in giving business leads and supporting businesses with their knowledge and experience. Even where your business is not limited by shares, you can still have an honorary board that can perform the role of backing your new business with their experience, knowledge and clout. You should also understand that an honorary board should not necessary be a formal board. It may just be a network of experienced business people you consult as a young entrepreneur among your contact.

START SMALL AND CELEBRATE EVERY SUCCESS: Starting small is the magic that breeds successful business. Every successful entrepreneur you have seen started as a small business. As a young entrepreneur, you must start with whatever capital or resource you have and work your way up by expanding from the bottom up. You must also remember to celebrate every little success you achieve on your journey and make little progress a morale boosting experience.

Anytime you make small progress, it becomes a foundation on which you can build more progress. This develops your confidence and desire to achieve, and make you confident enough to tackle your next task.

Success comes as a series of small steps not and not always as a big jump.

BE SEROUS WITH YOUR BUSINESS: People will take you serous based on the level of seriousness you attach to your business. When you have appointment at 5:30am, be sure to be there before 5:30am immaculately dressed and ready for business. If you your customer asked you to make a presentation and 12:00 noon, be there at 11:30am and not a minute late. If you demonstrate such qualities, your clients, partners and potential financiers will eventually notice your exceptional attitude to work and will shape their attitude towards you in the same regard.

UTILISE AVAILABLE RESOURCE AT YOUR SCHOOL: Universities and other higher institutions of learning are a fertile ground for acquiring knowledge both in business and academics. These institutions specialize in churning out professionals in every field and can serve as fertile ground to launch any startup.

The first resources available are your professors and lecturers, many of whom may be acting as consultant for other businesses operating outside the school. Some universities even have business incubation centers that are dedicated to churning out startups with dedicated support for small businesses. You can start by discussing your ideas with your academic supervisor and asking them for advice and input.

Another resource you can utilize is your academic research or thesis. These are usually a requirement for most first degree or higher degree programs. You must choose a research topic that will deepen your understanding of the business you intend to do and make you understand the market your business will serve better. For the young student entrepreneur, learning all you can about your new business should be a priority. Your new business should not only be a passion; it should also be your obsession. You should make it an extension of yourself and spend adequate time improving yourself and your business to deliver better results.

INTERNSHIP: Most students have opportunities to work as interns in established businesses during vacations. Your internship should serve as a very good opportunity to learn from an experience business and gain valuable knowledge on how to manage a successful business. To make the most of your internship program, ensure you choose a successful company that is in the same industry as the business you want to start. This will yield valuable experience and knowledge and also help you learn how your potential competitors successfully operates their business.

ACADEMIC RESEARCH: Most college and tertiary students are required to undertake some form of academic research as a requirement for their course. As a young entrepreneur, you must ensure you use this opportunity to learn as much as you can from your industry, market, potential clients, and how innovation can be deployed in your new business to achieve better result. Frederick W. Smith adopted this strategy by researching on how courier and delivery Service Company can be successful in the information age while studying at Yale University. His company FedEx is among the most successful courier companies in the world.

STEP 7

MAKE THE SALE

LEARN STRATEGIES TO SELL AND MARKET YOUR PRODUCT

For student entrepreneurs venturing into the business world, mastering the art of sales and marketing is as crucial as developing a groundbreaking product or service. This dual aspect of business not only drives revenue but also builds the foundation for long-term success and brand recognition. However, navigating sales and marketing can be particularly challenging for those balancing their entrepreneurial ambitions with academic responsibilities.

For your business to be grow and be sustainable, you must find client that will buy your product. Not only that, you must also ensure you are achieving progressive growth in sales. Without sales, your business will not survive. In other words, your business will collapse if you do not make enough sales.

UNDERSTANDING THE BASICS

At its core, sales involve direct interactions with potential customers to facilitate the exchange of your product or service for monetary value. Marketing, on the other hand, encompasses a broader set of activities aimed at understanding customer needs, building brand awareness, and creating demand for your offerings. In simple language, sales involve creating a relationship with your buyer. This relationship will ensure your client keep coming back to you for repeat business.

THE IMPORTANCE OF SALES AND MARKETING

For student entrepreneurs, excelling in sales and marketing is not just about immediate gains; it's about establishing a presence in your chosen market and building relationships with your customers. Effective sales strategies can lead to immediate revenue, which is crucial for the survival and growth of any start-up. When starting a new business, young entrepreneurs should adopt cost effective sales techniques that ensures least cost. Expensive advertisements and promotional activities should be avoided at all cost, except where such activities are leading to immediate and tangible sales. Below are sales strategies young entrepreneurs can adopt to sell the products.

SALES STRATEGIES FOR STUDENT ENTREPRENEURS

LEVERAGE PERSONAL NETWORKS

For student entrepreneurs, the journey from an innovative idea to a successful business venture is filled with unique challenges and opportunities. One often-overlooked asset is their network of personal relationships. Friends, family, classmates, and professors can not only offer support and encouragement but also serve as a springboard to market validation and initial sales.

Personal networks offer a trust-based platform that can be invaluable for early-stage entrepreneurs. This trust can lead to initial sales, constructive feedback, and word-of-mouth marketing, all of which are crucial for a new business. However, leveraging personal relationships requires a balance between professional persistence and respect for the personal connection.

Perhaps the most famous example of leveraging personal relationships is Mark Zuckerberg's initial launch of Facebook. Zuckerberg first introduced the platform to his fellow Harvard students, relying on the dense network of campus relationships to spread the word. The trust and relevance within this closed community helped Facebook gain rapid traction, demonstrating the power of starting with a familiar and accessible market.

Before Airbnb became a global phenomenon, founders Brian Chesky and Joe Gebbia tapped into their personal networks to find their first users and hosts. They started by renting out their own apartment and then reached out to friends and acquaintances to both list and book spaces. This initial use of personal relationships not only helped validate the concept but also built a foundation of trust and reliability that would become central to Airbnb's brand.

For student entrepreneurs, leveraging personal relationship also comes with lower cost compared to other sales method. This is significant considering most student entrepreneurs start with little or no capital.

FOCUS ON SOLUTION SELLING

In today's competitive market, simply having a good product is not enough. Successful entrepreneurs, especially those still in school, must understand the art of solution selling. This sales strategy focuses on identifying and solving the specific problems of potential customers rather than just pushing a product. For student entrepreneurs, who often have limited resources and brand recognition, solution selling can be a powerful way to build trust, differentiate from competitors, and ultimately increase sales.

Solution selling is about creating value for customers by understanding their unique challenges and offering solutions tailored to their needs. This approach requires deep knowledge of both the product and the customer's industry, pain points, and desired outcomes. By positioning their product or service as the answer to specific problems, entrepreneurs can make a more compelling case for why their offering is the best choice.

Melanie Perkins, a university of Australia student, identified a significant gap in the market while teaching design programs to fellow students. She found that many people found existing design software complex and intimidating. This insight led to the creation of Canva, an online design and publishing tool that simplifies the design process. Perkins and her team sold Canva as a solution to the problem of accessible design, catering not only to professionals but to anyone looking to create beautiful designs easily. Canva's solution-focused approach has made it a global phenomenon, with millions of users worldwide.

For student entrepreneurs, solution selling offers a strategic pathway to increase sales and build a loyal customer base. By focusing on solving real problems and tailoring offerings to meet specific needs, young entrepreneurs can stand out in a crowded market. The success stories of Melanie Perkins illustrate the effectiveness of this approach. Implementing solution selling requires a deep understanding of your customers, a commitment to addressing their unique challenges, and the flexibility to adapt your solutions as those needs evolve.

UTILIZE LOW-COST DIGITAL TOOLS

My advice for student entrepreneur is to always make your business a technology driven business from the start. It is always important to leverage on technology at the beginning of your business as it will help you save cost, and enable you to reach customers you will otherwise not reach.

Numerous digital tools and platforms can streamline sales processes, from customer relationship management (CRM) software to online payment systems. Many of these offer student discounts or free tiers for startups. Starting your business on a budget often means leveraging cost-effective digital tools to enhance productivity, marketing, communication, and management. Here's a list of some useful low-cost digital tools across various business needs.

a. COMMUNICATION AND COLLABORATION

- **SLACK**: a messaging app for teams that makes communication more organized and accessible.

- **MICROSOFT TEAMS**: useful for larger organizations using the Microsoft ecosystem, providing chat, video calls, and integration with office tools.
- **TRELLO**: a visual tool for project management, allowing teams to organize tasks with cards and boards.
- **ASANA**: helps teams track their work with projects, tasks, and deadlines.

b. MARKETING AND SOCIAL MEDIA

- **HOOTSUITE**: Manages multiple social media profiles, schedules posts, and analyzes social media traffic.
- **MAILCHIMP**: An all-in-one marketing platform that helps manage and talk to clients, customers, and other interested parties. Their marketing emails, automated messages, and targeted campaigns are especially useful.
- **CANVA**: A user-friendly graphic design tool with templates for creating professional-looking graphics for social media, presentations, and more.
- **BUFFER**: Streamlines the scheduling of posts across various social media accounts and offers analytics to track engagement.

c. SALES AND CUSTOMER RELATIONSHIP MANAGEMENT (CRM)

- **HUBSPOT CRM**: Offers a free version of its CRM tools, providing businesses with basic functionalities to manage relationships with customers.

- **ZOHO CRM**: Includes a free edition for small businesses with essential CRM functions and integration with social media.
- **SALESFORCE ESSENTIALS**: Provides a more robust CRM solution tailored to small businesses, though it comes at a low cost compared to the full Salesforce platform.

d. FINANCIAL MANAGEMENT
- **WAVE**: A free financial software designed for small businesses, supporting accounting, invoicing, and receipts.
- **MINT**: Helps with personal and business finance management, tracking spending, and creating budgets.
- **QUICKBOOKS ONLINE**: Offers various pricing tiers and is great for bookkeeping, accounting, and financial management.

e. PRODUCTIVITY AND ORGANIZATION
- **EVERNOTE**: A note-taking app that helps organize personal and professional projects.
- **GOOGLE WORKSPACE**: Includes Gmail, Docs, Drive, Calendar, and more—great for collaboration and productivity within a team.
- **DROPBOX**: Provides cloud storage solutions that simplify file sharing and data backup.

f. WEBSITE DEVELOPMENT AND E-COMMERCE
- **WORDPRESS**: A powerful, scalable platform for creating websites and blogs, with plenty of free and premium themes and plugins.

- **SHOPIFY**: An all-in-one commerce platform to start, grow, and manage a business, especially useful for creating and managing online stores.
- **WIX**: Provides an easy-to-use drag-and-drop website builder and customizable templates.

g. SEO AND WEBSITE ANALYTICS

- **GOOGLE ANALYTICS**: Offers insights into website traffic and marketing effectiveness, which is essential for digital marketing.
- **SEMRUSH**: Provides tools for SEO, pay-per-click, social media, and content marketing. The basic features are affordable, with more comprehensive features available at higher costs.
- **MOZ PRO**: An SEO toolset that provides data to increase traffic, rankings, and visibility in search results.

Using these tools effectively can help manage various aspects of your business more efficiently without breaking the bank. Each tool offers different plans and features, so it's worth exploring what fits best for your specific business needs and budget.

MARKETING TACTICS FOR STUDENT ENTREPRENEURS

HARNESS THE POWER OF SOCIAL MEDIA

In today's digital landscape, social media is more than just a platform for socializing; it's a powerful business tool that can drive brand awareness, increase sales, and create meaningful customer relationships. For student entrepreneurs, social media offers a low-cost, high-impact marketing avenue that is particularly useful when resources are limited.

Students entrepreneurs must start with the goal of building strong brand identities on social media. Creating a recognizable brand identity on social media can help establish trust and encourage engagement. This involves consistent use of logos, colour schemes, and messaging across all social media platforms.

Another way to harness social media is through content creation. Content is king on social media. Effective content not only attracts followers but also engages and convinces them to buy. This can include tutorials, behind-the-scenes videos, customer testimonials, and live Q&A sessions. Julie Deane started The Cambridge Satchel Company from her kitchen table with just £600. By creating compelling content that showcased the quality and fashionability of her satchels, she caught the attention of fashion bloggers and influencers, which eventually led to her bags being featured in high-end fashion magazines. Young entrepreneurs must use content to create affinity and better recommendation from their client. This can be achieved by encouraging customers to share their own photos and stories when using your product can provide social proof and attract new customers. This also fosters a community around your brand, and lead to more sales.

EMAIL MARKETING

Email marketing remains a potent tool for businesses of all sizes, providing an excellent return on investment and a direct line to potential customers. For student entrepreneurs looking to dip their toes into the world of business, leveraging email marketing can be an effective way to drive sales, build relationships, and establish a brand identity.

Email marketing is a form of digital marketing that involves sending emails to a group of people who have signed up to receive them. This method is used by businesses of all sizes to communicate with potential and existing customers. It's one of the most direct and effective ways of connecting with your audience, promoting your brand, and increasing sales. Here are some key elements and benefits of email marketing:

According to a study by the Data & Marketing Association, email marketing has an average return of $42 for every $1 spent, highlighting its efficiency and profitability. A survey by HubSpot reveals that 61% of consumers enjoy receiving promotional emails weekly, and 38% would like emails to come even more frequently, suggesting that well-crafted emails are not seen as a nuisance but as valued information. With over 4 billion daily email users, and expected to reach 4.6 billion by 2025 (Statista), the reach of email marketing is immense and growing, providing a broad audience for new entrepreneurs.

For student entrepreneurs starting with email marketing, there are several platforms that offers free plan for startups. I have listed some of the most effective and recognised platforms that offers free startup plans below.

MAILCHIMP: Ideal for beginners, Mailchimp offers a free tier that supports up to 2,000 contacts and 10,000 sends per month, which is more than adequate for most new ventures. It's user-friendly, with drag-and-drop email builders and predefined templates.

SENDINBLUE: Sendinblue free plan includes unlimited contacts and 300 emails per day, plus automation, which makes it perfect for those looking to get a little more sophisticated with their campaigns without a financial commitment.

CONSTANT CONTACT: While it doesn't have a free tier, Constant Contact offers a comprehensive solution with a user-friendly interface, extensive customer support, and a 60-day free trial, allowing you to test its features thoroughly.

CONVERTKIT: Designed with creators in mind, ConvertKit offers a specific set of tools for entrepreneurs who also produce content like blogs, podcasts, or videos. Their free tier includes up to 1,000 subscribers and basic features, which are excellent for content-driven campaigns.

Email marketing offers student entrepreneurs a unique combination of cost-effectiveness, broad reach, and direct engagement with customers. By understanding your audience, creating compelling and personalized content, and using the right tools, you can significantly enhance your business's ability to generate sales and grow sustainably. As you implement these strategies, keep tracking your results and refining your approach to find what best resonates with your target market.

COLLABORATE AND PARTNER

For student entrepreneurs, navigating the competitive landscape of business can be daunting. However, many young innovators have discovered that one of the most effective strategies to amplify their impact and increase sales is through collaboration and partnership. This approach not only broadens their market reach but also enhances their brand's credibility and resource pool.

Collaboration involves working with others to create something new or improve an existing process or product. For student entrepreneurs, this can mean partnering with peers, joining forces with larger companies, or even linking up with non-profits for mutual benefit.

Partners can share resources such as technology, expertise, and financial assets, which can reduce costs and increase operational efficiency. Collaborating with other businesses can open up new markets and customer bases. Each partner brings their own unique audience, potentially doubling the visibility of your product. Combining different perspectives and skills can also lead to new ideas and innovations, helping your business to stand out in a crowded market. When projects are shared, so too are the risks. This can be particularly appealing for student entrepreneurs who are risk-averse due to limited capital.

One of the most famous examples of student entrepreneurship collaboration is Facebook. Initially developed by Mark Zuckerberg and his college roommates Eduardo Saverin, Andrew McCollum, Dustin Moskovitz, and Chris Hughes at Harvard University. This collaboration not only leveraged their combined skills in programming, design, and business strategy but also their network of university contacts to spread the word and expand the user base rapidly.

For student entrepreneurs, collaboration and partnership are not just strategies for business growth—they are essential tools for survival and success in the competitive market landscape. By combining resources, sharing risks, and expanding market reach, students can transform their entrepreneurial ventures into thriving businesses.

STEP 8

RAISE CAPITAL

MOBILISE RESOURCE TO START AND GROW YOUR BUSINESS

Every entrepreneur must perform one core important function, which is bringing together the various factors of production in order to produce a given product or service. This is at the heart or the entrepreneurship function. Without this function, no product or service can be produced, and no profit can be made.

Bringing together the various factors of productions means finding the resource with which to start and operate the business. In order words, you are responsible for raising the startup capital and putting together the resource that are needed to start your new business. This can be a daunting task for many young entrepreneurs, even as it is for much experienced entrepreneurs.

LET START WITH MY BARE MINIMUM FUNCTION THEORY

Before we even discuss how you can raise startup capital, let discuss my concept of the bare minimum function. This concept will help you understand why you don't need large capital to start any business or why many successful global businesses started with very little capital yet were successful in business.

At the heart of every business is what I call the core functions. These are the activities and functions that earn money for the business. Around the core functions, there are desirable functions. Desirable functions add value to our core service and may be necessary to help us differentiate our products from other product. Around the desirable functions are the ostentatious functions which may not add any value to our product at all, but makes us feel good. Every entrepreneur must be able to differentiate between these three functional levels of activities and be able to tell which among them constitute his core functions.

When businesses are at the stage of bankruptcy, you can turn situation around by reducing activities to your core functions. This means cutting down cost whiles performing the core functions that earns the business money. This necessarily means identifying the ostentatious and desirable functions and making sure the business is not losing money by performing these functions, and ensuring these functions are reduced to their barest minimum. It means avoiding activities such as excessive printing and administrative cost, unnecessary travels, mobile and data expense or some labor cost. Some businesses may even undertake labor layoff and ensure they are operating with the bare staff they need to render their core services. Such business identifies their key staffs that are responsible for their core functions and operates with such staff. When businesses reduce their activities to their core functions, their cost of operation significantly reduces and they are able to steer their business to profit again if they consistently work on generating more revenue by attracting and retaining more clients. In many instances, businesses that are distressed financially can adopt this strategy and be able to stay in business till they return to making profit.

As a young entrepreneur, you must identify what constitute your core functions and concentrate on strengthening these functions. You must eliminate every unnecessary expense and operate like a company will do when in distress. Learn to operate on a lean budget and start your business with a lean capital. That is how all successful businesses start, and this is how they stay in business.

FOLLOW THESE 10 GUIDELINES WHEN SOURCING FOR FUNDS

Capital is an important element in the process of creating every successful startup. Whiles it does not determine how successful your startup will be alone, making sure you choose the right funding and ensuring that your funding is structured to suit the nature of your business can make the difference for a young entrepreneur. As a student entrepreneur, you must combine creativity with best practice and ensure you choose the best funding sources for your new business.

PLANNING IS KEY: It is important you don't just decide you need just about any capital to start a business. You must take time and think through the kind of business you want to start and the kind of funding that can best support that business. If you have any doubt about financial planning, ensure you consult an experienced mentor or financial advisor who can help you plan such as process.

CHOOSING THE RIGHT FUNDING IS AS IMPORTANT AS PLANNING: Not every funding will be good for your new business. As such, you must thoroughly consider the terms and conditions attached to every funding carefully and consider its long-term implication on your business. You must understand how your pricing, repayment frequency, installment amount or any form of security or equity you put up in exchange for funding can affect your business and ownership in the future. Attach much seriousness to such decisions and ensure you fully understand the implication of your choices before signing on any funding offer.

YOU MUST BE ABSOLUTELY PREPARED: Before you meet any potential investor to discuss funding your new business, it is important to be absolutely prepared and ready for any questions or concerns they may raise. Finding a potential investor that will be willing to sit down and listen to a young entrepreneur may be difficult enough in itself and should not be taken lightly. Be sure to prepare a brief 5 to 10-minute pitch that is very clear, concise and convincing. And don't forget to prepare a very good plan and financial projections that clearly demonstrate the competitive edge you will have over your competitors and the profitability of your new business.

AVAILABILITY OF FUNDING OR THE LACK OF IT SHOULD NOT DETERMINE THE SUCCESS OF YOUR BUSINESS: Not having large capital to start your new business does not mean your business will fail. Again, having abundance of it does not guarantee the success of your new business. Entrepreneurs must recognize the decision they make with what funding is available will account for the success they achieve. You must therefore ensure you don't make securing funding your main priority at the expense of having a good operational plan.

BE INNOVATIVE: most entrepreneurs tend to consider personal savings, loans from banks or friends as the avenues for raising capital which is far from the truth. Today's economy presents numerous opportunities for young entrepreneurs to secure funding for the business ideas. You should be open minded and explore other options such as venture capital financing, export promotion funds, angel funds and crowd-funding sources.

RESEARCH: There are a myriad of opportunities out there for young entrepreneurs. The key to securing the right funding is having a good, clear and convincing plan and knowing where to look. Student entrepreneurs should make sure to conduct a good research on funding before setting out to look for such funds. For students exploring to start their business with a small startup capital which I recommend, the internet may be a starting point to begin snooping around.

BEING PATIENT: it is important to also recognize that raising money will need time and patience. Every potential investor who shows any interest in financing your startup will like to do so at their own speed and time. You must demonstrate both confidence and patience and understand not every lead you follow will be successful.

YOUR BUSINESS IS NOT AN EXPERIMENT: This is one of the common mistakes you can ever make when sourcing for funds as a student entrepreneur. Many students will admit they are starting their business on part-time and will consider making it permanent when they graduate. In the mind of an investor, such mindsets are unacceptable. You must clearly demonstrate you are willing to stay on your business and make it succeed even if it doesn't progress as you wish whiles in school. An investor will only invest in your business if he/she is certain of your commitment and absolutely believe you will not abandon the business in which he has investment when you face a few challenges.

BE WILLING TO MEET CONDITIONS: No investor will make a condition-free offer to fund your business. Every funding lead you follow will come with its own demands, conditions and requirements. Common among these are the provision of financial statement, security, equity in exchange for funding and guarantors among others. Be ready and prepared to answer questions related to these and to also demonstrate how you will put the funds to use and how it will impact on your business.

DEMONSTRATE YOUR BELIEF: More than anything, your conviction, confidence and belief in your new business will affect investor decision to invest in your business. You must clearly demonstrate your belief that your business will be successful and highlight the sacrifice, commitment and capital that you have already invested in your business.

AVAILABLE OPTIONS FOR FINANCING YOUR BUSINESS

Two options are available to every entrepreneur when it comes to financing your business. Either you opt for equity funding or debt funding. All funding sources can be classified under one of these sources. When it comes to the actual details, some funding may even be structured to include both equity and debt funding at the same time.

EQUITY FUNDING

Equity funding/capital refers to the personal investment that the owners/founders makes. This is also risk capital as the owners assume the primary risk of losing their capital if the business is not successful. Equity funders become owners of part owner of the business and have a say in how the business is managed.

The best side of equity funding for a young entrepreneur is that it does not have to be repaid. Equity funders put up resource or capital to support your business in exchange for shares in the business. This allows the founder time to concentrate on making the business succeed. When the business succeeds, equity funders share in the profit and success of the business.

The major disadvantage for a young entrepreneur is the loss of full ownership. Sometime, the founder of the business may even end up with minority stake in the business. This is not necessarily bad as owning 40% of a successful business is better than 100% of failed business. Below are the options for equity funding.

PERSONAL SAVINGS: Young entrepreneurs should make saving for their business a major part of their lifestyle as this is the first option to look when considering equity funding. Personal savings from part-time jobs, student's loans, allowances from internship and money for upkeep from parents and relatives. It is also necessary for young entrepreneurs to put up the first round of startup capital as other investors and lenders will be interested in how much of their own resource they have invested in their business before investing in the business.

RELATIVES AND FRIENDS: For many young entrepreneurs, personal savings alone won't be enough to fund their business. If you are a young entrepreneur, there is even a greater chance you will need external funding beyond your personal savings. The next place to look for equity funding will be your close relatives, external family members and friend. My recommendation is to first discuss your new business and seek funding from your immediate parents or guardians. Parents can also give valuable advice on which relative to approach for funding. Relatives can also put up other logistics such as spare rooms or garages which can be used as an office for your new business. You should also consider your network of friends beyond your relatives as another source of equity funding.

PARTNERS: Forming partnership can also inject much needed funds into your startup in exchange for equity. A new partner may bring additional capital and resource that may not be available to you as a young entrepreneur. As with equity investor, you must also note that partners will want to a say or voice in how the company is managed.

ANGEL INVESTORS: Beyond putting up personal savings and support from relatives and family, businesses eventually outgrow this level of support. Angel investors can step in with much needed equity funding for startups with significant growth potential. Angel investors are simply high network individuals or wealthy entrepreneurs who invest in startups in exchange for equity stake in the business. Most angel investors are willing to invest in startups and young entrepreneurs whose business has significant growth prospects (even in their infant stages) long before banks and other commercial lenders will be willing to invest in such businesses.

VENTURE CAPITAL: Venture capital are private funding organizations or quasi-government agencies who identify and acquire equity stake in young business with growth and profit prospect with the hope of making gains when the business succeeds. Venture capital can provide much needed funds for startups to expand.

GOING PUBLIC: Successful companies may outgrow that level of funding the can receive from angels or venture capital funds. Such businesses can consider selling shares to the public in order to raise much larger capital for further expansion. It should be noted that going public comes with a lot of regulatory and stringent requirement and should be undertaken only after careful assessment of their impact on existing shareholders and investors. Also, not all companies will qualify or meet the conditions required for a company to go public. As such, startups cannot consider going public as an immediate or even short-term funding alternative.

DEBT FUNDING

Aside equity funding, the other major alternative to raising capital is by debt funding. The entrepreneur raises capital by accessing loans which are invested in the business. Debt capital allows the entrepreneur to maintain full ownership of his business but has the added disadvantage of debt repayment with interest. Before going for debt funding, the entrepreneur must consider several factors including the pricing, structure and terms of the facility being offered. The entrepreneur must also undertake cash flow analysis to ensure and borrowed capital can be fully repaid without default when making such a decision. Sources for debt funding are discussed below.

RELATIVES, FRIENDS OR PARTNERS: Before any decision is made by the young entrepreneur to opt for external debt capital, the first option that should always be considered should be close and extended relatives, friend and partners. Even the famous African entrepreneur Aliko Dangote who is ranked by Forbes as the richest man in Africa started with a loan of 500,000.00 Naira from an uncle. Students and young entrepreneurs must ensure they have fully explored all available options from family friends or partners before making any decision to source other forms of debt funding.

COMMERCIAL BANKS: Most commercial banks specialize in advancing short, medium and long-term loans to support entrepreneurs. Such loans are advanced with specific purpose and must be applied only for the purpose for which it is disbursed. Entrepreneurs that wish to access such loans must open and operates account with a commercial bank aside meeting other credit requirement. Such requirement may include satisfactory operation of account, providing specified financial statements, providing some form of collateral among others.

Most commercial banks have SME's banking units that specialize in supporting small and medium scale business. It is important to have early discussion with you bank in order to know what will be required of you should you need to access such a facility. Knowing the credit requirement of your bank does not necessarily mean you should access a loan. It will however help you prepare and help you appreciate the client-banker relationship better. Young entrepreneurs that are just starting their business may also find it difficult to meet such stringent requirement at first. In addition to that, I recommend startups opts for the first option of accessing loan from family and friends before considering doing so from commercial banks.

FINANCE COMPANIES/MICROFINANCE/NON-BANK FINANCIAL INSTITUTIONS: Non-bank financial institutions, microfinance or finance houses also provides debt capital for entrepreneurs. These companies are generally more risk tolerant and are able to serve markets which are often overlooked by traditional banks. Another advantage is their simplified and quick application process. Some finance houses, microfinance and non-bank financial institution are able to approve loan request within 48 hours from the time of application. This can be helpful to most young entrepreneurs that are not able to access credit from traditional banks. On the dark side, most microfinance and non-bank financial institutions adopt unorthodox approach to recovering loans from clients and I strongly recommend that young entrepreneurs seek professional advice before making a decision to approach finance houses. Loan from microfinance and finance houses are also come at significantly higher interest than commercial banks. Always consult and experienced mentor or financial advisor before choosing this option.

GOVERNMENT INTERVENTIONS: Government in most countries provides various state interventions that are aimed at financing and supporting entrepreneurs. The Ghana venture Capital Trust Fund, EDAIF, Youth Employment Agency, Business linkage Program all provides various supports for entrepreneurs. Other international

NGO's and donor sponsored agencies such as DANIDA, JICA, DFID and USAID may also have different interventions for supporting young entrepreneurs. Young entrepreneurs should be innovative in seeking funding and look beyond traditional funding sources. A simple online research and visit to agency offices can help young entrepreneurs to understand and apply for entrepreneurial support where possible.

WHERE TO START (FROM YOUR OWN POCKET)

Working within the Banking space for more than fifteen (15) years, I have come across several entrepreneurs with excellent business ideas who can't find any support simply because they have not invested in their own ideas. Let assume Mr. X come to me and want my bank to finance a new business to produce fruit juice. He makes an excellent business presentation and asks my bank to support his idea. The first question I will ask is how much of his resource he has invested in his business idea, or how much equity does he have in his own business? If his answer is none, then I am not interested.

As an entrepreneur, you must demonstrate you believe in your dream and are willing to take risk to make it succeed. This involves investing the first round of your own savings as capital before approaching other parties to invest in your business. This why young entrepreneurs must learn to save.

STEP 9

PREPARE A BUSINESS PLAN

DEVELOP A SUCCESS BLUEPRINT TO HELP YOU GROW YOUR BUSINESS

Planning is essential to running a successful business. This is an integral element that shapes business result but is often overlooked by most entrepreneurs. Many entrepreneurs start operating their business before sitting down to plan the details of what they want to achieve. Many will simply overlook this process when they achieve early success as they begin to spend more time on running the business. Without a clear plan and strategic direction however, short term success will be short-lived as market become more competitive.

Young entrepreneurs must learn to incorporate strategic planning into their business at their infant stage. This establishes a solid foundation on which long term success can be achieved. This chapter will guide you to develop a simple, clear, concise yet convincing business plan that can lay the foundation for enforcing short term success and achieving long term growth.

WHAT MAKES A SUCCESSFUL BUSINESS PLAN?

Several factors go into writing a successful business plan the most important of which is to ensure your plan speak clearly and can convince your target audience

PUT YOUR AUDIENCE FIRST: Never forget your plan is a selling document that will be read by different categories of people. If you are engineering student seeking to start an engineering business, avoid using engineering jargons that will confuse the rest of us, or make sure there is an appendix to explain complicated technical jargons when you need to use them.

You must also know clearly who you are targeting with your plan and ensure your plan satisfy their demand. If you intend to apply for a GHS500,000.00 from any bank, your plan should clearly indicate how the additional capital will be put into good use to achieve growth and profitability. Putting your audience first means penning your plan to sell your business in the most convincing way.

CAPTURE AUDIENCE WITH YOUR FIRST PAGE: No need to write long complicated intro lines. Your plan should explain clearly and convince anyone who read your first page what your business is about and what you want to achieve. Many entrepreneurs will make the mistake of putting their most important information in the middle of their plan. This is a grave error as potential investors may not read up to the middle page if your first two pages don't convince them. So, avoid the mistake of burying vital information in chapter 13 and ensure your first two pages summarize your plan and clearly tells your reader what the company intend to achieve in the short, medium or long term, and what the financier stands to gain by financing your business.

KEEP IT SIMPLE: Understand that a business plan cannot answer all questions an investor or lender will ask. Avoid congesting too much information into your business plan as a bulky plan may also put off investors from reading. Instead, maintain brief and clear section that gives valuable information about your business and causes potential investors to develop interest in your business. This will cause potential investor to invite you for further meeting where they will ask further questions after reading your plan. A good presentation or marketing pitch added to a business plan will convince potential investors to invest in your business.

SHOW COMPETITVE ADVANTAGE: Your business plan should highlight what set your business apart from other businesses. It should demonstrate the competitive advantage that differentiates your business from other businesses offering the same or similar product. Most importantly, it should directly inform potential investor about what is unique about your company. When penning a business plan, young entrepreneurs should demonstrate competitive advantage in four main areas; products, service, pricing and technology. This convinces potential investors your business can create value and gain market share when they invest in the business.

KEEP IT CURRENT: Assumptions and market demands underpinning business plans changes with time. It is therefore necessary to ensure business plans are revised when circumstances change or when the company assumes a new strategic direction.

MAKE IT RELEVANT: Most entrepreneurs only pull out their business plans when there is the need to visit a potential investor or their bankers. A business plan should be a document that defines broadly where you want to take your business. It should set clear vision and mission that will guide future actions. Employees and partners must also understand what the company values and be abreast with whatever plans the company has for the present and future. Again, your plan should be reviewed at the start of every

RESEARCH IS KEY: A good business plan thrives on having access to vital information about your product, market and competitors. Young entrepreneurs should take time to research their industry and acquire knowledge about the kind of business they want to start.

WRITING THE PLAN

A good business plan should be unique and not blindly resemble a general template or format. Young entrepreneurs should adopt all resource available such as info graphics, computerized spread sheets to produce business plans that is both demonstrative and informative. The following are common element of a successful business plan.

COVER PAGE AND TABLE OF CONTENT: As an official document, you must ensure your Business Plan comes with a cover page and a table of content. The cover page should come with the name of the company, logo, and contact information and date of publication.

EXECUTIVE SUMMARY: Your executive summary briefly describes the most important and relevant point in your business plan. This should be convincing enough to cause the reader to want to read your business further. There is no need burying most important information in page 10 which prevents readers from showing any interest in your plan after reading the first two pages. The executive summary must clearly state what you want, what the business hopes to achieve and what competitive advantage the business has over other competitors.

For our hypothetical fruit juice business, good example or an executive summary is provided below. Note how we speak directly to our lenders about our product acceptance, increasing demand and the need to expand.

VISION AND MISSION STATEMENTS: Entrepreneurs must develop a clear vision and translate it into a meaningful mission statement that can inspire employees, partners and investor to help achieve their vision. A vision statement should paint a compelling picture of where the company wants to go and serve a source of direction for business strategy. A good mission statement should encompass the three elements of *purpose* of the company, the *business* it does and *values* it cherishes.

BRIEF COMPANY HISTORY: It is important to let investors and financiers know the history behind your business. This should give information and when and how the company was formed, and highlight any special events such as acquisition of new equipment, signing of key agreements etc.

BUSINESS AND INDUSTRY PROFILE: The business and industry profile present a short or brief description of the industry and present both its present and future outlook. Investor will like to know if there is a positive outlook for your industry. Ensure you point or explain clearly increasing demand for your kind of product and present statistics to show how consumer demand is expanding in your industry where possible.

BUSINESS STRATEGY: Entrepreneurs must present what strategy and approach they will adopt to beat their competitors. They can do this by presenting any method or approach they will adopt to counter their competitors, what kind of delivery, speed and service innovation they will deploy to make their business stand out from their competitors.

MARKET STRATEGY: Every industry has what consumers' lookout for when making decisions to buy. Entrepreneurs must conduct extensive market research and analysis that identifies the unique demographic of their market and use the information to craft a well-informed marketing strategy they will adopt to penetrate their market. The marketing strategy is of key concern to potential investors and lenders as it will determine whether the product will be successfully received buyers and consumers.

COMPETITOR ANALYSIS: A good competitor analysis will help you determine the strength and weaknesses of competitors within your market. Sampling competitor's product and asking potential client to share their like or dislike about these products can help you design a marketing strategy that takes advantage of their weaknesses. You can use this information to develop a brand that will be well received by the market, including competitor's client.

MANAGEMENT PROFILE: Next on your business plan is the management profile, which introduces the management team to your potential investors. Potential investors and lenders always take a keen interest in your level of experience when making a decision to invest or not to invest in your company. Unfortunately for most student entrepreneurs, this area represents one of their greatest weaknesses. Students entrepreneurs may not have many years of experience or may even lack experience at all which comes as a risk to most investors. Again, students who are still in school may not have completed their course yet and therefore have not earned the necessary qualification in the strict sense. It is hence necessary for the student entrepreneur to ensure this section of their business plan sufficiently address these concerns and assures potential investors or lenders of their ability to succeed in their chosen business.

When writing the profile of key managers, student must emphasize and the key skills they bring to the new business. Key knowledge and skills that has enabled them to succeed in the business should be given significant mention. Another strategy young entrepreneurs can adopt is to include experienced board or honorary board members at the profile section of the business plan (This should be done obviously with the consent of the board members). Many members may come with several years of experience that can easily assuage the concern of potential investors about your lack of experience.

OPERATION AND MANAGEMENT PLAN: Next on your business plan is to present an organogram/organizational chart that depicts the key roles in your organization. The operations and management plan describe how the business functions on a continuing basis and present key positions in the organization and the qualification that are required to fill these roles.

FINANCIAL STATEMENTS: This section of the business plan presents the financial projection for the business. Financial statements give information about the performance of your business, and also indicate where your business should be. For existing business, banks will want to know how your businesses have performed within the last three years. If the business has been in operation for a year, then present financial statements these years in the business plan. The three main kind of financial statements that should be included in the Business Plan are the Income Statements, Cash Flow Statements and the Balance Sheets.

THE BALANCE SHEET

In a simple language, a balance sheet shows what your company is worth in a particular year. It is therefore usually prepared at the last day of the year (31st December). A balance sheet has two major sections which are the assets (showing everything that the company owns) and the liabilities and equity section (which shows which proportion of the assets is owned by creditors and which proportion is owned by the company owners).

A balance sheet must also agree with the accounting equation: Assets (A) = Liabilities (L) + Owner's Equity (E). Any increase in one side of the balance sheet must be offset with either an increase or decrease at the other side of the balance sheet to ensure agreement with this accounting equation. Let take a brief look at what appears on the balance sheet.

ASSETS: The balance sheet presents all assets of the company. Assets are the resources owned by the business. This gives an idea of the value of all assets owned by the business. When preparing the balance sheet, assets are usually grouped under current asset, non-current assets or fixed assets.

LIABILITIES: liabilities refer to the company's obligations, debts or any claim against the company aside the owners' equity. Liabilities are classified into current liabilities and non-current liabilities. Current liabilities are those debts that must be repaid within one year or within the normal operating cycle of the business. Non-current liabilities or long-term liabilities are those that must be repaid after a year.

EQUITY: The final part of the balance sheet is the equity section which contains all contribution made by the business owners to support the business. This part of the balance sheet also contains all accumulate earning retained by the owners and reinvested into the business.

THE INCOME STATEMENT/PROFIT AND LOSS ACCOUNT

The income statement, or profit and loss statement (P&L), reports a company's revenue, expenses, and net income over a period of time. It does this by comparing the company's revenue to it cost thus given an overview of the company's profitability over the given time period. The purpose of the income statement is therefore to help managers understand if the company made profit or loss, and how the profit/loss was incurred. The major parts of the income statement are stated below.

REVENUE: The revenue section of the incomes statement presents the total revenue/sales the company accrued over the period against the cost of generating the revenue/sales. By calculating the difference between revenue and its cost, we derive the gross profit which gives an indication of the profit margin the company makes on selling its products. This section may also include other revenue such as interest income or revenue from selling company's assets.

OPERATING EXPENSE: Operating expense includes all administrative, marketing and labor expense the company incurs during the stated time period. The company operating expense must be deducted from gross profit to enable it arrive at operating income for the period.

TAXES: The income statement also accounts for the company's tax obligation by deducting total tax paid over the period from operating income.

STATEMENT OF CASH FLOW

The statement of cash flow reports the cash the business generates during the stated time period and how it was used by the business. In other words, the cash flow statement shows the changes that occur in the working capital of the business as it operates from the beginning of the year to the end of that year (or any time period stated). Many creditors or potential investors may require the cash flow statement which makes it imperative for small businesses to prepare this report.

CASH FLOWS FROM OPERATING ACTIVITIES: This part of the cash flow statement presents the actual cash the company received from its operations. This is usually the net income or net profit declared in the income statement/profit and loss statement in the previous operating year.

CASH FLOW FROM FINANCING ACTIVITES: Next is to add other sources of the company's funds. Notable among them are external funding from banks or lenders, floating of the company's shares, funding by partners. Since the objective of the cash flow statement is to give a comprehensive indication of the flow of cash within the company, and funding the founder is able to secure from relatives, partners or friends should also be recorded in this section.

CASH FLOW FROM INVESTING ACTIVITIES: Companies also make investment outside their business which may lead to interest income or loss. Such moneys should appear in their statement of cash flow under the investing activities section.

CREATING PROJECTED FINANCIAL STATEMENTS

Many startups and small businesses may not have convincing records of past performance to show to potential creditors or investors and need to go beyond presenting financial statement for the current year. This means they must make some assumptions about their sales and use their forecast to project the kind of profit they expect to generate in their financial projections. Young entrepreneurs who have already started their business will have an idea about their sales and can rely on their experience to forecast the sales they are likely to make over the period.

Let use our Nkwa Fruit Juice as an example. Let assume our Nkwa brand only sells two flavors of juice; Pineapple Juice and Orange Juice. We sell our juice in 1Liter bottles for GHS 5.00 (five Ghana cedis which is sold by the supermarket for GHS 8.00). We are currently supplying 15 supermarket outlets in Accra with each outlet buying 100 Liters of each flavor per month. This means for our Pineapple brand we will sell 1,200 Liters per year to each supermarket. Since we supply to 15 different supermarkets in Accra it means in a year, we will sell a total of 18,000Liters of Nkwa Pineapple Juice and 18,000.00Liters of Nkwa Orange Juice. This mean our annual total revenue from Nkwa pineapple Juice will be GHS90,000.00 (18,000Liters x GHS 5.00) and same for Nkwa Orange Fruit Juice. Therefore, our projected annual revenue for Nkwa Fruit Juice Limited will be GHS 180,0000.00 (GHS 90,000.00 from Nkwa Pineapple Juice and GHS90,000.00 from Nkwa Orange Fruit Juice)

This assumption should be the starting point for preparing your projected financial statement. It is important to note that even though your financial statements are projections, there is the absolute need for it to be based on reality. You must ensure your projected sales are realistic and not overly optimistic.

NOW LET COME BACK TO OUR NKWA FRUIT JUICE BUSINESS

Remember we said at the beginning of this book we will be starting a fruit juice supply business called Nkwa Fruit Juice Limited. We have completed step six and are ready to prepare the business plan for our new company. I have used the assumption I made above to develop a abridged yet forceful business plan you can use to sell your business to a new investor. You can use the same steps we have used in this book to develop your own business plan for any business you want to start. After completing your business plan, your next step is to register your business with is briefly covered as the final step in this book

NKWA FRUIT JUICE LIMITED

Location: 2nd Floor, Greenwich Tower, Tema
Website: www.richardannan.com
Email: achieve@richardannan.com
Contact: 024 XXX XXXX

BUSINESS PLAN

15TH JAN, 2024

EXECUTIVE SUMMARY

Nkwa Fruit Juice Limited produces 100% Natural Fruit Squeeze with no added artificial preservative or sugar. The company started in February 2015 with operation covering only Tema metropolis. With early success, the company has increased its sales outlet from initial 3 to 15 and now supplies supermarkets in Accra and Tema.

Due to the increased demand for its products, the company plans to expand to cover the whole of the Tema and Accra and has signed distribution agreement with two major outlets and is having ongoing discussion with other outlets which will increase its sales revenue by more than 100%.

The company has so far operated with internally generated fund by its owners. To be able to meet increasing demand and also carry out planned expansion, the company is seeking a capital injection loan of GHC 150,000.00

MISSION STATEMENTS

To become the leading source of naturally produced fruit beverage in Ghana by providing 100% premium quality product to our clients.

VALUE STATEMENTS

Our values can be the summarized with the mantra 'customer first, quality first'.

We shall place the health and interest of our cherished client first and be dedicated to serving our client with products of the highest quality standard.

COMPANY HISTORY

Nkwa Natural Fruit Juice is owned by Richard Annan and J. Annan who started selling the fruit squeeze in their Tema Community 1 neighborhood in February 2015. After initial success, the two finally decided to expand the business in September 2015 and started supplying supermarkets around Tema.

From this humble beginning, Nkwa Fruit Juice can now be bought at 15 major supermarkets in Tema. The company has three staff with plans to employ two additional staff due to increased demand for its products.

The company has also signed a supplier's agreement to supply RJA Superstore and JA Trading Limited which together has a chain of 15 supermarkets across the country.

BUSINESS AND INDUSTRY PROFILE

GLOBAL FRUIT JUICE MARKET:

The global market for fruit and vegetable juices is forecast to reach 64.46 billion liters by the year 2015, encouraged by steadily increasing emphasis on health and nutrition. Fruit and Vegetable juices continue to exist as one of the most competitive segments in the beverage industry competing strongly against RTD drinks, sports & energy drinks and bottled water.

Despite being hit by the global recession, the market will pick up pace over the near term, powered by gains made from natural juices, fortified juices and juices made with healthier ingredients.

GHANA FRUIT JUICE MARKET:

There is increasing Consumption of fruit juice in Ghana which has become popular and increasing daily. Consumer awareness of the benefits of consuming sugar free naturally blended juice is pushing the demand for fruit juice which reached which reached USD 231.30 million in 2023. The market is further expected to grow at a CAGR of 5.8% between 2024 and 2032, to reach a value of USD 386.51 million by 2032.

The domestic market for fruit juices has become strong in part because Ghanaian consumers increasingly appreciate the natural taste and health benefits of Ghana's own agricultural products. It is believed that Fruit juices are the most consumed beverage next to water, however approximately 70% of these juice products are imported. According to estimates, 10.4 million litres of fruit juice is consumed yearly.

Ghana's location offers conditions that are close to optimum for growing tropical fruits which will ensure regular and constant supply or raw materials for the fruit juice market. The country is endowed with an assortment of fruit, including mangoes, pineapples, citrus and coconut among others. The opportunity to transform agricultural produce into juice and other value-added consumer products for domestic and foreign markets, and ultimately dominate the processed fruits industry exist, but few local companies have taken advantage of this opportunity.

BUSINESS STRATEGY

Nkwa Natural Fruit Juice will concentrate on generating strong sales performance in Greater Accra region with special emphasis on the city of Tema and Accra. The company will expand operations to other regions of Ghana after fully exploiting opportunities in the Greater Accra Regions.

SALES STRATEGY

We will drive sales for our product by providing direct sales personnel to sell our product at each of our distribution outlet. This is necessary as our brand is an emerging brand compared to competitors that have greater name recognition advantage. This strategy will push sales at all our distribution centers and ensure we achieve our sales target for each month.

COMPETITOR ANALYSIS

The Fruit Juice Market is currently saturated with foreign imported brands which account for about 70% of the market. Local fruit juice brands such as Blue Skies, Kalyppo, and Tampico account for the remaining 30% of the market.

Most imported Fruit Juice brands have added preservative and coloring which will give Nkwa Natural Fruit Juice which is a 100% natural fruit juice with no added preservative an advantage.

To differentiate our brand, Nkwa Fruit Juice will market itself market itself as the 100% Natural Fruit Juice with no added sugar and preservative. The company shall also actively participate in community-based events in Greater Accra such as student hall weeks and festivals to advertise our brand.

OPERATION AND MANAGEMENT PLAN

Nkwa Natural Fruit Juice Limited is currently managed by Richard Annan who founded the business in 2015 and has successfully expanded the business to cover Tema and part of Accra. In order to ensure sustained growth, the company is set up to directly focus on customer needs and sales.

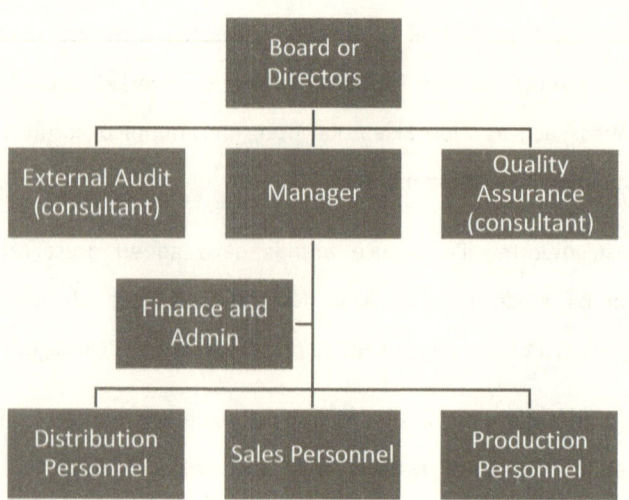

FINANCIAL STATEMENTS:

NKWA FRUIT JUICE COMPANY LIMITED

5 YEAR FINANCIAL PLAN

PROFIT AND LOSS PROJECTIONS

		Year 1	Year 2	Year 3	Year 4	Year 5
Revenue						
	Gross revenue	$648,000	$660,960	$687,398	$728,642	$786,934
	Cost of goods sold	291,600	297,432	309,329	327,889	354,120
	Gross margin	$356,400	$363,528	$378,069	$400,753	$432,814
	Other revenue [source]	$0	$0	$10,000	$0	$0
	Interest income	$1,000	$0	$0	$0	$0
	Total revenue	$357,400	$363,528	$388,069	$400,753	$432,814
Operating expenses						
	Sales and marketing	$2,000	$2,040	$2,122	$2,249	$2,429
	Payroll and payroll taxes	60,000	$61,200	$63,648	$67,467	$72,864
	Depreciation	20,000	20,400	20,800	21,200	21,600
	Insurance	1,500	$1,530	$1,591	$1,687	$1,822
	Maintenance, repair, and overhaul	15,000	15,300	15,600	15,900	16,200
	Utilities	6,000	$6,120	$6,365	$6,747	$7,286
	Property taxes	5,000	$5,100	$5,304	$5,622	$6,072
	Administrative fees	3,000	$3,060	$3,182	$3,373	$3,643
	Other	3,200	$3,264	$3,395	$3,598	$3,886
	Total operating expenses	$115,700	$118,014	$122,007	$127,843	$135,802
Operating income		$241,700	$245,514	$266,063	$272,910	$297,011
	Interest expense on long-term debt	12,065	4,800	(0)	(0)	(0)
Operating income before other items		$229,635	$240,714	$266,063	$272,910	$297,011
	Loss (gain) on sale of assets	0	0	1,000	0	0
	Other unusual expenses (income)	0	0	0	0	0
Earnings before taxes		$229,635	$240,714	$267,063	$272,910	$297,011
Taxes on income	18%	40,186	42,125	46,736	47,759	51,977
Net income (loss)		$189,449	$198,589	$220,327	$225,151	$245,034

NKWA FRUIT JUICE COMPANY LIMITED

5 YEAR FINANCIAL PLAN

BALANCE SHEET PROJECTION

Assets	Initial balance	Year 1	Year 2	Year 3	Year 4	Year 5
Cash and short-term investments	$50,000	$338,081	$479,438	$744,564	$1,039,415	$1,231,050
Accounts receivable	3,000	3,000	3,000	3,000	3,000	3,000
Total inventory	25,000	25,000	25,000	25,000	25,000	25,000
Prepaid expenses	0	0	0	0	0	0
Deferred income tax	0	0	0	0	0	0
Other current assets	5,000	5,000	5,000	5,000	5,000	5,000
Total current assets	$83,000	$371,081	$512,438	$777,564	$1,072,415	$1,264,050
Buildings	$0	$0	$0	$0	$0	$0
Land	100,000	100,000	100,000	100,000	100,000	100,000
Capital improvements	0	0	0	0	0	0
Machinery and equipment	100,000	100,000	100,000	100,000	100,000	100,000
Less: Accumulated depreciation expense	0	20,000	40,400	61,200	82,400	104,000
Net property/equipment	$200,000	$180,000	$159,600	$138,800	$117,600	$96,000
Goodwill	$0	$0	$0	$0	$0	$0
Deferred income tax	0	0	0	0	0	0
Long-term investments	0	0	0	0	0	0
Deposits	0	0	0	0	0	0
Other long-term assets	0	0	0	0	0	0
Total assets	$283,000	$551,081	$672,038	$916,364	$1,190,015	$1,360,050

Liabilities	Initial balance	Year 1	Year 2	Year 3	Year 4	Year 5
Accounts payable	$2,000	$2,000	$3,000	$3,000	$1,500	$1,500
Accrued expenses	0	0	0	0	0	0
Notes payable/short-term debt	0	0	0	0	0	0
Capital leases	0	0	0	0	0	0
Other current liabilities	100	100	100	100	100	100
Total current liabilities	$2,100	$2,100	$3,100	$3,100	$1,600	$1,600
Long-term debt from loan payment calculator	$50,000	$28,632	($0)	($0)	($0)	($0)
Other long-term debt	$100,000	$200,000	$150,000	$175,000	$225,000	$150,000
Total debt	$152,100	$230,732	$153,100	$178,100	$226,600	$151,600
Other liabilities	0	0	0	0	0	0
Total liabilities	$52,100	$30,732	$3,100	$3,100	$1,600	$1,600

Equity	Initial balance	Year 1	Year 2	Year 3	Year 4	Year 5
Owner's equity (common)	$50,000	$50,000	$50,000	$50,000	$50,000	$50,000
Paid-in capital	250,000	250,000	250,000	250,000	250,000	250,000
Preferred equity	0	0	0	0	0	0
Retained earnings	0	189,449	388,038	608,364	833,515	1,078,550
Total equity	$300,000	$489,449	$688,038	$908,364	$1,133,515	$1,378,550
Total liabilities and equity	$352,100	$520,181	$691,138	$911,464	$1,135,115	$1,380,150

NKWA FRUIT JUICE COMPANY LIMITED

5 YEAR FINANCIAL PLAN

CASH FLOW PROJECTIONS

	Year 1	Year 2	Year 3	Year 4	Year 5	Total
Operating activities						
Net income	$189,449	$198,589	$220,327	$225,151	$245,034	$1,078,550
Depreciation	20,000	20,400	20,800	21,200	21,600	104,000
Accounts receivable	0	0	0	0	0	0
Inventories	0	0	0	0	0	0
Accounts payable	0	1,000	0	(1,500)	0	(500)
Amortization	0	0	0	0	0	0
Other liabilities	0	0	0	0	0	0
Other operating cash flow items	0	0	0	0	0	0
Total operating activities	$209,449	$219,989	$241,127	$244,851	$266,634	$1,182,050
Investing activities						
Capital expenditures	$0	$0	$0	$0	$0	$0
Acquisition of business	0	0	0	0	0	0
Sale of fixed assets	$0	$0	($1,000)	$0	$0	(1,000)
Other investing cash flow items	0	0	0	0	0	0
Total investing activities	$0	$0	($1,000)	$0	$0	($1,000)
Financing activities						
Long-term debt/financing	$78,632	($78,632)	$25,000	$50,000	($75,000)	$0
Preferred stock	0	0	0	0	0	0
Total cash dividends paid	0	0	0	0	0	0
Common stock	0	0	0	0	0	0
Other financing cash flow items	0	0	0	0	0	0
Total financing activities	$78,632	($78,632)	$25,000	$50,000	($75,000)	$0
Cumulative cash flow	$288,081	$141,357	$265,127	$294,851	$191,634	$1,181,050
Beginning cash balance	$50,000	$338,081	$479,438	$744,564	$1,039,415	
Ending cash balance	$338,081	$479,438	$744,564	$1,039,415	$1,231,050	

STEP 10

REGISTER YOUR BUSINESS

COMPLETE ALL LEGAL REQUIREMENT FOR YOUR BUSINESS

Many entrepreneurs start working on their business long before they register such businesses. In reality, your business never really becomes recognized until it is fully registered. Young entrepreneurs must ensure they fully satisfy every legal requirement of their business in terms of registration and operation.

When deciding on registering your business, it is necessary to understand the different forms of business ownership and the advantages and disadvantages of each form of ownership. Generally, entrepreneurs make this decision after several considerations. The forms of ownership are Sole Proprietorship, Partnership, Limited Liability Company. This chapter briefly discusses the disadvantage and advantages of each form of ownership.

it should be noted that this chapter doesn't fully exhaust the topic of business ownership as other types of ownership still exist aside the one mentioned. The Joint venture, Limited partnership, Corporation and Non-Governmental organization are other forms of business owner that should also be understood by the entrepreneurs.

THE SOLE PROPRETOR

The Sole proprietor is the simplest and most popular form of business ownership. It is also the least costly form of business to start. As the name implies, a sole proprietor is a business that is owned and managed by one individual

BENEFIT OF REGISTERING AS A SOLE PROPRIETOR

EASY TO REGISTER: Sole proprietor is very easy to register and is also the simplest form of business to create. Since the business is owned by one person, bureaucratic processes are short and making decisions is much easier.

COST LESS TO REGISTER: Sole proprietorship is the least costly form of business compared to other businesses forms.

NO PROFIT SHARING: Since a sole proprietor is the single owner and manager of his business, he gets to keep all the profit from the business after paying all statutory taxes. This is a major advantage as such profit can be retained to expand the business.

EASY TO EXIT: A sole proprietor is the originator, owner and manager of his business. Should there be any need to discontinue the business, he can do so quickly without having to discuss with partners or other shareholders.

LESS BUREACRATIC TO OPERATE: Sole proprietor has less legal requirements to meet and is the least regulated form of business among all forms of business types.

AUTONOMOUS DECISION MAKING: Sole proprietor is autonomous in taking decisions about their business. He can therefore respond quickly to events and take advantage of short-term opportunities. Sole proprietor therefore has the freedom to take important decision about their business without having to consult partners or shareholders.

DISADVANTAGE OF THE SOLE PROPRIETOR

PERSONAL LIABILITY: the biggest disadvantage of operating as a sole proprietor that it comes with unlimited personal liability. This simply means the owner is personally liable for the company's debts. Your creditors are allowed to hold you personally liable for all the company's debt should your business collapse. Apart from forcing the sale of the company's asset, creditors can also force the sale of the owner's personal asset to offset any loan the owner may have incurred whiles running the business.

LIMITED CAPACITY: A sole proprietor must rely on his own capital, knowledge and skill which limit him in terms of capacity and result achieved. It is rare to come by an entrepreneur who has mastered all skills and can work all by himself without external help or support. Since such perfect entrepreneurs do not exist, Sole proprietorship are limited by their weakness which becomes the weakness of the business they manage.

ACCESS TO CAPITAL LOW: Generally, lending to a one-man business is considered to be riskier than lending to other forms of business. The sole proprietor may therefore face difficulties in attracting large capital which may intend stifle the growth of the business. The Keyman risk occurs when a business or business unit becomes heavily reliant on a key individual(s). Although this risk is found is other forms of business including large corporations, it is very common with Sole Proprietors who operates self-owned businesses.

LACK OF CONTINUITY: A sole proprietor owns and manages his business alone. In many cases, the owner is the face and soul of the business, possessing the skills which enable the business to function. When business owner passes away or is incapacitated, it may mean the sudden end of the business.

THE LIMITED LIABILITY COMPANY

As the name suggest, a Limited Liability Company offers possible protection against lawsuit for the owners. A Limited Liability Company is a private company whose owners are legally responsible for its debts only to the extent of the amount of capital they invested. For young entrepreneurs seeking to start a business with the intention of growing such businesses, a limited a liability company offers a better platform to grow your business and attract outside investors. Owners of LLC are only liable to the extent of their investment in the company, whiles their personal assets are not considered to be an extension of the company by default.

ADVANTAGES OF LIMITED LIABILITY COMPANIES:

LIMITED PERSONAL LIABILITY: One of the most significant advantages of forming an LLC is the limited personal liability it provides to its owners. In an LLC, owner's personal assets are typically protected from business debts and liabilities. This means that if the business faces legal action or financial troubles, creditors generally cannot pursue the personal assets of the members to satisfy business debts.

FLEXIBILITY IN MANAGEMENT: LLCs offer flexibility in management structure compared to sole proprietor. Owners can choose to manage the company themselves or appoint managers to handle day-to-day operations. This flexibility allows for a more customized management approach that suits the needs and preferences of the owners.

CREDIBILITY AND PERPETUAL EXISTENCE: Operating as an LLC can enhance the credibility of a business, as it signifies a formal legal structure. Additionally, unlike sole proprietorships and partnerships, LLCs have perpetual existence, meaning that the business can continue to operate even if one of the owners leaves or passes away.

DISADVANTAGES OF LIMITED LIABILITY COMPANIES:

COSTS AND FORMALITIES: Starting a limited liability company comes with more costs associated with formation, including filing fees compared to starting a sole proprietor. Additionally, some countries require annual fees and filings fees to maintain the LLC's good standing, which can add to the ongoing costs of operation.

TAX COMPLEXITY: Limited liability companies has a more complex tax requirement compared to sole proprietorship, especially as the business grows. Depending on the number of owners and the distribution of profits, tax implications can become more intricate, requiring careful planning and potentially the involvement of tax professionals.

COUNTRY-SPECIFIC REGULATIONS: LLCs are subject to country-specific regulations, and the laws governing them can vary significantly from one country to another. This can create challenges for LLCs operating in multiple countries or looking to expand their operations beyond their initial jurisdiction.

POTENTIAL FOR MEMBER DISPUTES: Like any business structure involving multiple owners, LLCs can be susceptible to disputes among owners and directors. Differences in management style, decision-making, and financial goals can lead to conflicts that may disrupt business operations and require resolution through legal means.

PARTNERSHIP

Partnership is a form of business ownership where two or more individuals join forces to run a business together, underpinned by partnership contract. It offers a middle ground between sole proprietorship and limited liability company, providing advantages and disadvantages unique to its structure. Understanding these aspects is crucial for young entrepreneurs considering this route.

ADVANTAGES OF PARTNERSHIP:

SHARED RESPONSIBILITY AND EXPERTISE: One of the primary benefits of partnerships is the ability to share responsibilities and leverage the diverse expertise of each partner. Partners can pool their skills, knowledge, and resources to manage different aspects of the business effectively. As a young entrepreneur, having the right partners can help you mitigate several disadvantages such as inexperience, lack of expertise and access to funding.

FINANCIAL STRENGTH: Partnerships often enjoy greater financial strength compared to sole proprietorships. With multiple partners contributing capital, the business can access more funds for investment, expansion, or overcoming financial challenges.

RISK SHARING: In partnerships, risks are distributed among the partners. This shared risk can provide a sense of security for individual partners, as they are not solely responsible for bearing the burden of losses or liabilities.

DISADVANTAGES OF PARTNERSHIP:

UNLIMITED LIABILITY: One significant disadvantage of partnerships is unlimited liability. Each partner is personally liable for the debts, obligations, and actions of the business, including those incurred by other partners. This puts personal assets at risk and can lead to financial ruin if the business encounters legal or financial trouble.

CONFLICT AND DISPUTES: Partnerships are susceptible to conflicts and disputes among partners, which can arise due to differences in opinion, work ethic, or management styles. Disagreements over business decisions, profit sharing, or the direction of the company can strain relationships and hinder business operations.

SHARED PROFITS: While partnerships allow for the sharing of cost, this also means that profits must be divided among the partners according to the terms of the partnership agreement. Disputes may arise if partners feel that their contributions are not adequately reflected in the distribution of profits.

DEPENDENCY ON PARTNERS: Partnerships rely heavily on the participation and commitment of each partner. If one partner becomes incapacitated, loses interest, or leaves the business, it can disrupt operations and strain the remaining partners' resources.

WHERE TO START

Beyond the Sole proprietor and Limited Liability Company, young entrepreneurs can also explore other forms of ownership such as partnership, joint ventures and not for profit Organizations. Each of these comes with its own distinctive advantages and disadvantage and should be clearly understood before a decision is made to register any such businesses

SUBSCRIBE TO MY FREE PERSONAL COACHING AT

RICHARDANNAN.COM

Congratulations for reading the '10 Steps to Become a Successful Student Entrepreneur'. You have demonstrated a strong desire to learn and be successful as a young entrepreneur. If you need further resource and information on how you can succeed as a young entrepreneur, then visit richardannan.com and sign up for Richard's free Personal and Business Growth Webinars.

It will be a pleasure to assist and support you to start your success journey. Join me at richardannan.com and let's achieve success together.

Thank you.

Richard Annan
Speaker I Author I Entrepreneur I Business Executive

www.ingramcontent.com/pod-product-compliance
Lightning Source LLC
Chambersburg PA
CBHW020431220526
45464CB00002B/650